Reading
and
Writing
Nonfiction Genres

WITHDRAWN

Kathleen Buss
University of Wisconsin–Stevens Point
Stevens Point, Wisconsin, USA

Lee Karnowski
University of Wisconsin–River Falls
River Falls, Wisconsin, USA

INTERNATIONAL
Reading Association
800 Barksdale Road, PO Box 8139
Newark, Delaware 19714-8139, USA
www.reading.org

The International Reading Association attempts, through its publications, to provide a forum for a wide spectrum of opinions on reading. This policy permits divergent viewpoints without implying the endorsement of the Association.

Director of Publications   Joan M. Irwin
Editorial Director, Books and Special Projects   Matthew W. Baker
Senior Editor, Books and Special Projects   Tori Mello Bachman
Production Editor   Shannon Benner
Permissions Editor   Janet S. Parrack
Acquisitions and Communications Coordinator   Corinne M. Mooney
Assistant Editor   Charlene M. Nichols
Administrative Assistant   Michele Jester
Editorial Assistant   Tyanna L. Collins
Production Department Manager   Iona Sauscermen
Supervisor, Electronic Publishing   Anette Schütz
Senior Electronic Publishing Specialist   Cheryl J. Strum
Electronic Publishing Specialist   R. Lynn Harrison
Proofreader   Peggy Mason

Project Editors   Tori Mello Bachman and Shannon Benner

Cover Illustration   Margaret Scott

Library of Congress Cataloging-in-Publication Data
Buss, Kathleen.
    Reading and writing nonfiction genres / Kathleen Buss and Lee Karnowski.
        p.   cm.
Includes bibliographical references (p.) and index.
    ISBN 0-87207-346-7
1. English language—Composition and exercises—Study and teaching (Elementary)
2. Language arts (Elementary)   3. Prose literature—Study and teaching (Elementary)
I. Karnowski, Lee.   II. Title.
    LB1576.B955 2002
    372.62'3—dc21

                                                                                2002009343

Dedication

In memory of our fathers,
Frank Telepak and James Legters,
for teaching us the joy of nonfiction.

Contents

Acknowledgments

We would like to thank all the teachers and university students who have taught the reading and writing lessons, have collected the student samples, and have given us helpful feedback. In particular, we would like to thank Kristen Novitch and Lowie Schultz at Midway Elementary School in Gleason, Wisconsin, USA, for their help. We also would like to acknowledge Arlene Schulze, literacy consultant for the Merrill School District in Wisconsin, USA, and instructor at the University of Wisconsin–Stevens Point, USA. Her feedback on the genre lessons was very insightful.

Our thanks go to the children and families who willingly shared writing samples with us.

We also would like to acknowledge the help of the staff at the Red Balloon Bookstore in St. Paul, Minnesota, USA, for their aid in selecting books for the lessons and the Children's Literature Bibliography in this book. We also appreciate DeAn Krey, a colleague, for sharing her large collection of social studies children's books.

We would also like to say thank you to Kathleen's husband, Bruce Buss, and to Lee's friend, Linda Melcher, for their patience, encouragement, and genuine interest in our work. They kept us organized, fed, and entertained when we needed it the most.

To our friends at the International Reading Association, thank you for your wisdom, insight, and support. We are grateful to Matt Baker, Editorial Director of Books and Special Projects, who brought cohesiveness to our first drafts. A special thank you goes to our editors, Tori Bachman and Shannon Benner, for their considerable attention to the content of our book.

Educators agree that in order to lead elementary students to competence in literacy, teachers need to expose them to a wide range of literary genres. Educators also have agreed on the general terms *narrative* and *expository texts* to separate this range of genres, but these categories are not helpful in understanding the great variety of text structures found within each genre.

Narrative texts follow a text structure referred to as *story grammar*, or *story structure*. Story grammar includes the setting, characters, initiating event, subsequent events, and the final event, including the resolution. But story grammar does not explain the differences between fables, fantasy, or folk tales. Buss and Karnowski (2000) explain that the literary elements within a story grammar shape narrative genre. For instance, a folk tale has a setting, but it is a backdrop setting and not important to moving the story along. A folk tale has characters, but these are flat characters who are not richly embellished by the storyteller. The differences found in story grammar allow for the richness and creativity within narrative genres. Discussing the elements in texts has helped educators feel successful with the teaching of narrative text structures.

Graves (1994) states, "Nonfiction is an important genre for helping children and ourselves to know an area particularly well. In this sense, nonfiction is probably the most usable kind of writing for school and a lifetime of work" (p. 313). We feel that students will benefit from wide exposure to nonfiction texts. Many educators, however, have not felt the same sense of success in teaching nonfiction texts that they feel when teaching narrative texts. One reason may be that nonfiction text, unlike narrative text, has many text structures. For example, the text structure of game rules is much different from that of ABC informational books, and these two genres are different from cycle books—even though all these text structures are organized sequentially. Perhaps another reason for educators' lack of success teaching nonfiction texts is that they place too much emphasis on the structure of expository texts rather than on the authors' purpose in writing these texts. It does seem logical, however, that in their experiences with these texts, if students understand the authors' purpose, they can visualize how the text should be organized.

British and Australian researchers have tried to bring instruction of nonfiction texts to a level that educators can successfully take into the classroom (see Lewis & Wray, 1995; Lewis, Wray, & Rospigliosi, 1995; Wing, 1991). These researchers discuss *genre theory*, which according to Lewis and Wray, promises that "texts (written or spoken) are structured according to their purpose, and texts with the same purpose will have the same schematic structure" (p. 21). Lewis and Wray comment on the societal aspects of written language by stating, "It is in the context of a certain society that we have a purpose for creating a text, and that purpose gives rise to a text produced in a particular genre" (p. 22). These researchers agree, therefore, that purpose—or why the text was written—determines structure. Think of it this way: Why would we write down a recipe? Our purpose in writing a recipe might be so others can follow the steps and replicate the dish. Knowing the purpose when reading and writing helps us to understand what should be included or what our text structure should look like. For a successful recipe, we must have a name of the dish to know what we are making, and we must have a complete list of ingredients and detailed instructions for making this dish. On the other hand, why would we write down rules for a game we enjoy? Our purpose might be so others could play the game fairly time after time. Once we know the purpose, we understand what to include and what our text structure will be. For successful game rules, we need to state the object of the game, name the equipment used to play the game, give the number of players needed, and describe step by step how to play the game.

Using the purpose of expository text to teach students in grades 2–6 how to read and write nonfiction has led us to write this book. We feel that if nonfiction is taught to elementary students with an emphasis on purpose, the structures of particular types of nonfiction texts will fall into place. Students will then gain a better idea of text types, and they will be able to read and write them more effectively.

An Explanation of This Book's Organization

To identify the purpose for writing a particular text, we have drawn from opinions of researchers in the field. Bomer (1995) has identified nonfiction according to six purposes of the text: (1) to persuade readers, (2) to inform readers about something interesting, (3) to take readers on a journey of ideas, (4) to inform readers who are seeking information, (5) to show readers how to do something, and (6) to involve readers in a story. Lewis and Wray (1995) go a step further by identifying six categories of nonfiction text that are appropriate for elementary students: (1) recount, (2) report, (3) procedural, (4) explanation, (5) persuasive, and (6) discussion.

For this book, we have selected four genres of nonfiction text based on purpose:

1. Recount—to share a personal experience
2. Procedural—to show how to do something or how something works
3. Informational—to share information
4. Persuasive—to present an opinion or an argument

Within these four genres based on purpose, we have identified specific nonfiction subgenres that share a purpose. The genres that you select to present in your classroom will depend on your students' prior knowledge and the curriculum.

We have organized this book into six chapters around these four purposes of nonfiction text. We begin our discussion of teaching nonfiction genres with discussion of recounts in chapter 1. We purposely have started our discussion of nonfiction with recounts because many subgenres of recounts already are familiar to students in grades 2–6. Most young students have received and written letters, have kept personal journals, and have written personal stories and diary entries. In this chapter, we extend this existing personal knowledge by introducing recounts of others—biographies—and personal recounts—memoirs.

Chapter 2, Teaching Procedural Texts, includes two types of text: (1) those written to instruct and (2) those written to explain. In procedural text intended to instruct, the author guides or informs the reader how to do something; examples include rules for playing a game or directions for arriving at a destination. For procedural text intended to explain, the author explicitly and understandably details a process to achieve a specific goal; examples include recipes, first aid instructions, or operating guidelines. In this chapter, to teach both types of procedural texts, we have designed instructional strategies for teaching recipes and game rules.

In chapter 3, Teaching Sequentially Ordered Texts, instructional strategies for reading and writing ABC books and cycle books are shared. The author of sequentially ordered text describes a sequence of events in a logical order. In this way, the structure provides the scaffolding that helps the reader recall these events.

Chapter 4, Teaching Informational Texts, presents instructional strategies for reading and responding to texts such as books, brochures, guidebooks, and maps, all of which lead students to reading and writing reports and travel brochures. These texts are excellent guides for report writing, and as students experiment with the purposes of informational writing—to define, to describe, to present problems and possible solutions, to identify cause and effect, and to present information—they can model the authors' style. Reading and writing travel brochures sets the stage for students' understanding of descriptive passages.

Chapter 5, Teaching Journalistic Texts, explores nonfiction texts by crossing over into journalism. We realize the importance of being informed, knowledgeable members of a society, and newspapers supply this needed information for each of us to stay current in community, state, country, and world news. In this chapter, we have identified two very different purposes for journalistic writing: A human interest article is researched and written *objectively* by a reporter to give readers an account of an interesting person or recent event; an advice column is written *subjectively* by a columnist who gives recommendations to readers.

In chapter 6, Teaching Persuasive Texts, we investigate the power of writing that is intended to persuade or to argue a position, or point of view. We begin the teaching of persuasive texts using classified advertisements, a genre familiar to most students. We extend this discussion by exploring other types of persuasive texts such as editorials, letters to the editor, persuasive letters, speeches, and persuasive informational books.

This book explores the presentation of what nonfiction writing looks like and the purposes, structures, and literary elements inherent in nonfiction genres. We use teacher modeling and student discussions as the primary instructional strategies for presenting these structures and elements. As Wing (1991) writes, "Modeling enables the teacher to focus the children's attention on different writing forms and to develop a shared language to use when they interact with these texts" (p. 6).

Each chapter in this book begins with a description of the purposes for and forms of a particular nonfiction genre, followed by suggestions of books for you to use for a read-aloud session. Each chapter also builds background knowledge of how purpose is related to text structure, and each contains a suggested strategy for building background knowledge. Moss (1995) states that "nonfiction read-alouds allow children to experience the magic of the real world—of predators and their prey; of planets and oceans; of other lands, times and places" (p. 122). During read-alouds, not only do students gain invaluable knowledge from nonfiction books, but they also are exposed to the text structure of these books. Through this exposure, students begin to develop expectations of how authors craft their pieces while presenting factual information to their readers (Pappas, Kiefer, & Levstik, 1990).

The chapters of this book provide minilessons that encourage students to explore both text structures and literary elements. These minilessons can be introduced during the read-aloud or before the read-aloud as students become immersed in looking at texts within the chosen genre and begin to identify those elements and structures.

Modeling will continue as you help students understand the structure with a graphic organizer designed specifically for the genre being presented; blank examples of each graphic organizer can be found in Appendix A. During the read-alouds, you will ask students to fill in the graphic organizers using the information from the read-alouds. This modeling supports students as they learn about a new structure.

Finally, we suggest that students craft their own pieces using all they have learned in the minilessons and read-aloud discussions, thus linking reading and writing. We feel that writing is an excellent way to demonstrate an understanding of each genre and also involves students in the real purpose for which these pieces are written—to share information with an audience. In each lesson, student writing should follow the writing process: prewriting, drafting, revising, editing, and publishing. The graphic organizers used during the read-aloud may be enlarged and reproduced for use during prewriting to help students organize their information. A sample written by an elementary student has been included with each genre study in the book.

Finally, an extensive Children's Literature Bibliography is provided at the end of the book. It is organized according to chapter and subgenre so you can match books other than the read-aloud suggestions in the chapters with your curriculum or students' interests. All read-aloud books used in the chapters are cited under their respective classification in this bibliography.

We feel that introducing the study of nonfiction genres by classifying the genres according to purpose will aid students in their understanding of how authors craft nonfiction text. In this book, we have presented a balanced approach to teaching that starts with building students' background knowledge of the genre followed by guided lessons for reading and writing the genre. As students' awareness of nonfiction text expands, and as their understanding of the importance of seeking information from others and sharing information with others develops, we hope they will come to appreciate the variety of purposes and text structures of nonfiction. Moreover, we hope students feel confident reading, writing, and sharing these texts with others.

Chapter 1

Teaching Recounts

In a recount, an author writes a retelling or interpretation of an event or a series of events that are memorable in his or her life, or in the life of another person. A recount is a written restructuring or interpretation of an event or series of events. Lewis and Wray (1995) state, "Recounts are written to retell events, with the purpose of either informing or entertaining—or even with both purposes!" (p. 30). Recounts involve the reader in true experiences and events that have taken place.

Examples of recounts include biographies, autobiographies, memoirs, personal journal or diary entries, and personal letters. A *biography* is an account of one person's life written by someone other than that person. A biography can be written about a historic figure, someone who is living now or has lived during the lifetime of the author, or an ordinary person. It can be a full or partial account of this person's life organized in chronological order called a *lifeline*. As the biography progresses, events that happened during this person's life are shared.

An *autobiography* is the life of a person written in his or her own words, with events organized in a lifeline structure. An autobiography can be written by anyone who decides to tell the story of his or her life.

A *memoir* is an interpretation of a life event. Unlike an autobiography, when writing a memoir, the author selects one event or one aspect of his or her life to share with others. Zinsser (1987) states, "the writer of a memoir takes us back to a corner of his or her life that was unusually vivid or intense" (p. 21). Calkins (1994) notes, "in writing memoir, we select moments that reveal our own experiences of our lives" (p. 407).

Personal journals or *diary entries* are a special kind of recount in which individuals write about the events in their lives. In journals or diaries, writers decide their own topics and usually present events one day at a time. Although we would not normally take personal diary or journal entries through the writing process in the classroom, if they are meant to reach a larger audience, they can be revised and edited in class before publishing.

Personal letters contain personal recounts of events in a person's life that he or she wishes to tell special people who are far away. Letters are written to communicate with an interested audience, such as friends or family members. The friendly letter format can be used when teaching this type of recount writing.

Subgenres of recounts include the following:

All About Me books	partial biographies
autobiographies	personal journals/diaries
biographies	personal letters, memos, notes, postcards
eyewitness accounts	personal narratives
memoirs	reflections
memories	résumés
obituaries	sociological biographies

In this chapter, we will discuss the teaching of biographies and memoirs in detail. We feel that students in grade 2 would enjoy reading and writing "All About Me" (Tompkins, 2000) autobiographies, personal letters or postcards, and personal journal entries. Students in grades 3–6 would enjoy biographies, and students in grades 4–6 would be successful investigating memoirs.

General Recount Minilessons

General recount minilessons are brief, focused lessons that teach strategies for reading and writing recounts. They can be used before or during the reading of most recount texts.

Strong Verbs—Past and Present Tense

Recounts are usually written in past tense because the author is writing about past events, although a few memoirs are written in the present tense. Discuss with students the difference between past- and present-tense verbs, and the importance of using strong verbs in writing.

In the biography *Pioneer Girl: The Story of Laura Ingalls Wilder* (Anderson, 1998), strong past-tense verbs describe the many moves that the Ingalls family made:

> As Laura grew older, more and more settlers crowded into the Big Woods. Pa wanted to be where neighbors were not so close and wild animals roamed free. So on Laura's seventh birthday, Mary, Laura, and Carrie were once again bundled inside the covered wagon. As they drove away, they saw their little log house for the last time. They headed west, to the wide, open prairies of Minnesota. (n.p.)

In the memoir *Night Driving* (Coy, 1996), the author remembers accompanying his father on trips to the mountains. In the following excerpt, Coy tells about his memories in the present tense so we feel part of the night drives:

> As we drive, Dad unscrews the cap of his thermos.
> "Can you take the wheel?"
> "Sure."
> I watch the lines and steer straight while Dad pours coffee. (n.p.)

In the memoir *Up North at the Cabin* (Chall, 1992), the author concentrates on the verbs to show what she did and what she saw when she went to the cabin. These are also strong present-tense verbs:

> Like a house on stilts,
> a bull moose stands in the shallows.
> His chest heaves and rumbles,
> mighty as a diesel engine.
> I clutch the tow rope,
> bobbing up and down in my yellow life vest.
> The motor sputters softly, waiting.
> My legs stiffen in the skis. (n.p.)

Time-Related Words

Explain to students that events of recounts usually flow in chronological order, and time-related words help the reader visualize the progression of events over time. For example, in the memoir *Century Farm: One Hundred Years on a Family Farm* (Peterson, 1999), the author writes about his century-old farm, describing how some things on the farm have changed and some things have remained the same from one generation to another. Peterson uses time-related words to explain how his grandfather worked the farm, and how Peterson works the farm today:

> Every spring, Grandpa plowed the soil and seeded oats, rye, and barley. (n.p.)
> Each planting season still starts when I plant alfalfa and corn in the same old dirt. (n.p.)
> In late summer, Grandpa harvested the grain with a horse-drawn binder. (n.p.)
> Today, I harvest grain from the same fields with a machine called a combine. (n.p.)

Great Adjectives

Tell students that in order to help the reader visualize the events in a recount, it is important to use powerful words that paint a picture in the reader's mind. For example, in her memoir *Back Home* (1992), G.J. Pinkney uses strong adjectives to describe Uncle June: "He also had the same sparkling eyes and apple-dumpling cheeks as Grandmama Zulah in Mama's old photograph" (n.p.).

A.D. Pinkney uses strong adjectives to describe Bill Pickett's adventures as a cowboy in her biography *Bill Pickett: Rodeo-Ridin' Cowboy* (1996):

> One afternoon Bill was straddling the gate as usual when he spotted an eye-popping sight. A bulldog was holding a restless cow's lower lip with its fangs. Bill moved closer to get a good look at how the dog's bite kept the squirming cow down....
>
> Word of Bill's fearless riding spread from ranch to ranch. On Sundays folks gathered at local barnyards to watch Bill snatch a fire-eyed steer by the horns. (n.p.)

Strong Beginnings

Young readers may put aside a recount that does not capture their interest right away. Therefore, explain to your students that to capture readers' interest, the author uses a strong beginning or lead. This lead sets the stage for the action in the recount. Give students a variety of memoirs and biographies, and have them find strong leads. These leads may be in the form of a quotation, a description of a setting or character, an anecdote, or a question to help the reader relate to the recount. The following are some leads that encourage readers to continue reading.

The biography *And Then What Happened, Paul Revere?* (Fritz, 1973) begins with a detailed description of the historical setting:

> In 1735 there were in Boston 42 streets, 36 lanes, 22 alleys, 1,000 brick houses, 2,000 wooden houses, 12 churches, 4 schools, 418 horses (at the last count), and so many dogs that a law was passed prohibiting people from having dogs that were more than 10 inches high. (p. 5)

Lincoln: A Photobiography (Freedman, 1987) begins with a description of Lincoln and an anecdote:

> Abraham Lincoln wasn't the sort of man who could lose himself in a crowd. After all, he stood six-feet four-inches tall, and to top it off, he wore a high silk hat....
>
> At first glance, most people thought he was homely. Lincoln thought so, too, referring once to his "poor, lean, lank face." As a young man he was sensitive about his gawky looks, but in time, he learned to laugh at himself. When a rival called him "two-faced" during a political debate, Lincoln replied: "I leave it to my audience. If I had another face, do you think I'd wear this one?" (p. 1)

Building Background Knowledge of Recounts

Students will be reading a variety of recounts. As they read, they will be looking for the purpose of a specific text and identifying the text structure. The teaching strategy ARC (Vaughn & Estes, 1986), which stands for anticipation, realization, and contemplation, helps build background knowledge about recounts. In the anticipation phase of the lesson, the students are asked to use prior knowledge to predict the information that will be shared in the book. For example, share titles of memoirs, biographies, autobiographies, diary accounts, or collections of letters and ask students to predict what sort of information and what text structure they will encounter in this recount. In the second phase, realization, as you read aloud or as the students read recounts, ask the students to revisit their predictions and to revise or add to these predictions based on the knowledge they have received from the text. The last phase in this strategy is contemplation, which will be used as a building block to the actual writing of recounts later in the lesson. During the contemplation phase, ask students to predict what authors will share and what structures they will use to write other recounts of this genre. During contemplation, students should start thinking of writing their own recounts.

For example, during the anticipation phase, you might share *Louisa May Alcott: Her Girlhood Diary* (Ryan, 1993). Students may anticipate that the diary accounts will be about a writer, a person who lived a long time ago, a child, and the author of *Little Women*. Students might also predict that the recount will be organized by dates.

In the realization step, students will add information as they read this book. They may add information about events (such as Alcott's mother read to her, Alcott was a tomboy, and she had a temper), and students may have noticed other text features of diaries (such as the text is written in first person).

In the contemplation step, students will look at other recounts that follow the diary format and predict, based on reading *Louisa May Alcott*, what the other books will be like. For instance, before they read the next diary account, they should be able to predict that the text structure will be the same: dated entries, information both trivial and important, first-person account.

Teaching the Subgenre of Biography

The general minilessons presented at the beginning of this chapter and the ARC strategy will help students read and write biographies. Finding information and citing references are also helpful as minilessons specific to biographies.

Finding Information

Biographies written for children in the 1950s and 1960s were not inviting reads. The language was stilted, characters were too good to be true, and there was always a lesson for the reader about how to live life. These days, however, there are wonderfully engaging biographies for elementary students to read. The authors of these biographies carefully research the subject's life, and they tend not to make up any information, not even dialogue. In an article titled "Research Tells the Story"

(1996), Fritz describes how she writes biographies, then describes her research for the biography of Patrick Henry:

> This is research: reading, reading, reading both primary and secondary sources. Much may be repetitive but don't lose patience. Reading the same material over and over immerses you deeper into your subject and into the period…. (n.p.)
>
> At the end of my reading, I went to Virginia to retrace Patrick's steps. I visited all the homes that Patrick had lived in. I waded in the stream where he had fished; I sat under the tree where he liked to play his fiddle. (n.p.)

Students can be accurate biographers also. Explain that they can use two kinds of sources of information in their research. Primary sources include interviews of the subject, reading his or her diaries or letters, looking at photographs of the subject and his or her family, or talking with people who knew the subject. Secondary sources include books, videos, the Internet, and newspaper articles about the person.

George Washington's Breakfast (Fritz, 1969) demonstrates how to find information from primary and secondary sources. In this biography, George, a young boy who shares the same first name as his favorite president, wants to know what George Washington ate for breakfast. His grandmother says she will cook it for him if he can find out. George begins his search at the school library, where he and the librarian first check the encyclopedia, then use the card catalog to find biographies of George Washington. None of the books have the answer. George then goes to the Smithsonian Institution in Washington, D.C., and to Mount Vernon (Virginia, USA), but he does not find the answer. Instead of giving up, though, George goes up to his attic to think. There he notices a box of old books, and he finds the answer to his question in a book titled *The American Oracle* published in 1791.

Citing References in a Bibliography

The writing of children's biographies has become very sophisticated. Explain to students that many biographies include a bibliography, which is a list of sources such as books, articles, or other resources that the author used when writing the text. Sometimes the author refers to these resources in the text, so it is helpful for readers to have the information about the resource, in case they want to read more about the subject.

Ask students to look at bibliographies in biography books and make some judgments about how to create a bibliography. For instance, students may notice that the author's last name appears first, the names are in alphabetical order, and the title of the book is italicized. Explain that the city given is the place the book was published and the publishing company's name comes next. Each entry also includes the date when the book was published, or the copyright date. Although there are variations in the format of a bibliography, introduce and stay with one format, and when students write their biographies, have them list the books they use in their own bibliography.

An annotated bibliography gives all the information listed above, as well as a short description of the source. What follows is an example of an annotated bibliography entry from Russell Freedman's *The Wright Brothers: How They Invented the Airplane* (1991).

> Crouch, Tom D. *The Bishop's Boys: A Life of Wilbur and Orville Wright.* New York: W.W. Norton, 1989.
> A recognized authority on early aeronautics and the Wright brothers, Crouch emphasizes their family background, their personality traits, and their attitudes toward life and work. (p. 123)

A bibliography also can be used to find other books on the subject students want to research. Explain this so students understand that there is no one definitive study of a famous individual.

Reading the Biography

Before the class biography read-aloud, share with students that a biography is an account of one person's life written by someone other than the subject. It should not be a dry retelling of the events of this person's life, but a chronicle of surprising, interesting insights. Explain that authors can write about someone famous or someone ordinary. Authors can write a full biography about the whole person's life or authors can write a partial biography about one significant event. Discuss how a biography is different from a fictional story. Share with students that an author must never make anything up. It is important to research the person's life using primary and secondary sources.

To begin the study, select and read a biography to your class. The biography you select will depend on the age of your students. There are many excellent biographies for all ages. Although any biography can be used (see Children's Literature Bibliography), in this section we will discuss *Pioneer Girl: The Story of Laura Ingalls Wilder* (Anderson, 1998).

During or after the shared read-aloud, explain that authors follow certain elements that are included in the text. First, there is an introduction. In the introduction, the author gives us a time frame for this biography. The person's birth, birthplace, and family structure are explained. In our read-aloud, the introduction is as follows:

> Long ago, in 1867, when America was a land of dense forests and wide, open prairies, a pioneer girl named Laura Ingalls was born. She lived with her Pa and Ma and her older

sister, Mary, in a little log house among the big trees of Wisconsin. Laura's earliest memories were of her Pa and Ma packing everything they owned into a covered wagon. In went all their clothes, dishes, bedding, and books, and Pa's fiddle. Laura's family left the little house and traveled for days and weeks. They were going to Kansas. (n.p.)

Authors then give the details of the person's life, usually providing specific dates for events. Finally, authors provide a conclusion that results in a satisfying ending. The graphic organizer in Figure 1 shows an example of one filled in by students as they follow the read-aloud. Students also can fill in Graphic Organizer: The Biography (see Appendix A, page 92) as they read biographies on their own.

Figure 1   Example of the Biography Graphic Organizer

Introduction:		
Birth	Setting	Family
1867	midwest United States	Pa; Ma; older sister, Mary; younger sister, Carrie

Events:

1. Pa built a house on the prairie.

2. They returned to Wisconsin.

3. At 7, the family traveled to Minnesota.

4. They lived in a tiny one-room house.

5. They moved again to run a hotel in Burr Oak, Iowa.

6. They moved to the Dakota territory.

7. When she was 15, Laura became a teacher.

8. In 1885, she married Almanzo and she had a daughter.

9. In 1894, Almanzo and Laura moved to Missouri.

10. In 1915, Laura traveled to San Francisco, California.

11. When she was past 60, Laura wrote her first book.

12. In 1949, Almanzo died.

13. In 1957, Laura died.

Conclusion:
"I'm glad if my books have helped the children," Laura said when people praised her stories. She was pleased that she had done what she had set out to do: to tell the tales of the American pioneers for children everywhere and always. (n.p.)

Writing the Biography

Tompkins (2000) writes that a biography can have a sociological approach in which "the writer describes what life was like during a historical period, providing information about family life, food, clothing, education, economics, transportation, and so on" (p. 228). Before writing their biographies, ask students to select a person they know whose life events they might want to write about. Or, students may wish to write a biography about a person in their town who lived a long time ago, which would allow students to discover what life was like in their town then.

The writing of a sociological biography will follow the process of writing: prewriting, drafting, revising, editing, and publishing. Students can fill in Graphic Organizer: The Biography (see Appendix A, page 92) as a prewriting exercise for their biography. Students will need to first decide a subject for their biography. They will then need to figure out what they would like to know about this person, and draft a list of questions to ask the person if he or she is alive or questions to ask others about this person if he or she is not living. Students should practice interviewing with peers in the classroom prior to the interview of their primary source. Experiences in taking notes and recording direct quotes will help when the actual writing process begins. (See chapter 4 for more discussion of taking brief notes; see chapter 5 for more on using quotes.)

One third-grade teacher wanted her students to understand what their community was like 50 years ago. The teacher felt that an authentic way to learn about the community was to interview residents who had lived there at least 50 years. Students brainstormed questions that would allow them to learn about life 50 years ago. They then put these questions into categories, which could be used for the paragraphs of their biographies. The following are the questions the students used:

What is your full name?

What is your maiden name? (for women only)

How long have you lived in River Falls?

What year did you move to River Falls?

Where was your first home in River Falls?

How many siblings were in your family?

How many were older and younger than you?

Tell us about your schooling.

Where did you go to school?

When did you go to school?

How was school different than it is today?

What were the clothes like that you wore at home, at school, and for special occasions?

What kind of food did you eat when you were growing up?

How was it prepared?

What did you do with your time when you weren't in school?

What were some of your chores?

What toys and games did you play with?

As an adult, what did you do to earn a living in the community? If you stayed at home, what did your spouse do for his or her job?

What changes have you seen in our community?

What do you like best about our community?

Tell me about your most special memory.

After conducting her interview, Sami, a third grader, wrote the following biography:

Alpa Sroos Stone

Alpa Sroos Stone has lived in River Falls for 54 years. Her first home here was on the campus on Cascade Street. She moved to River Falls in 1946 with her mother, father, her two sisters, and her three brothers. Compared to her brothers and sisters, she was the youngest. Her family rented a home from the college on Cascade Street. Just imagine living in a small house with five siblings, a mother, and a father.

School was very different back then. Alpa Sroos Stone had to walk or skate 10 blocks to her school. She went to school in Valley City, North Dakota. She went to school around 9:15, Monday, Tuesday, Wednesday, Thursday, and Friday. She did not go to school in River Falls.

Alpa wore special clothes for special days. For home she wore dresses, long underwear, and shoes that went up to the bottom of her knee. For school, Alpa wore dresses, long underwear, and sometimes, if Alpa was lucky, she got to wear her big sister's clothes. When Alpa dressed up she wore her Christmas dress with woolshally.

Potatoes were on the menu when Alpa ate her meals. Every meal Alpa had potatoes to eat. Peeled, boiled, you name it—potatoes were at every meal. Brothers, sisters, mother, and father, all of them ate potatoes.

When Alpa wasn't in school, she was doing something else. Whether it was summer, winter, spring, or fall, Alpa took walks. In the winter, though, she went skating and sledding. One of the things Alpa hated most was doing chores. She had to help wash the dishes, make the bed, sweep the floor, and sometimes maybe even cook.

Some games Alpa played were croquet, Old Maid, Flinch, and sometimes for fun she would tip an outhouse. Other times she would go to the movies for $.10, or watch the neighbor children.

Alpa's job before she got married was a physical education teacher; her favorite thing to teach was basketball. She taught for 7 years, until she got married. Her husband was a teacher, too.

Alpa has seen many changes over the years. When she and her family came here, there were no houses to rent. She said the roads have changed, and there are now more cars. Alpa remembered that there are more schools now. And she also said that if you wanted a library, you had it in your house.

When I asked Alpa what she liked best about River Falls, she said her favorite was the college. She said that it is cheaper, easier, and much better. She also said that now more people get to go to college.

One of Alpa's favorite memories was on Halloween. It all started when she and her friend were trick-or-treating. Back then, kids thought it was funny to tip outhouses. When Alpa was looking at all the tipped outhouses she noticed one that was standing up. Then Alpa said, "That one is an easy one to tip." But the person who owned it heard her. But Alpa didn't know and had just walked away. Later that night someone tipped it but it wasn't Alpa. The next morning the woman came to Alpa's house and said, "Your sons need to come put up my outhouse because your little girl tipped it." But, Alpa didn't.

When writing a biography, an author has the liberty to choose a portion of a person's life and explore it in depth. This is a partial biography. Examples of partial biographies include *Bloomers!* (Blumberg, 1993); *Abe Lincoln Grows Up* (Sandberg, 1985); and *Why Don't You Get a Horse, Sam Adams?* (Fritz, 1974). One fifth-grade student, Kelsey, wrote a partial biography about an aspect of her mother's life, the keeping of a family horse. What follows is her partial biography about her mother, Carole; her brothers and sisters; and their horse.

Horsing Around

In 1974 Carole, Kathleen, John, Margaret, and Thomas King got a horse. They named the horse Papoose. They kept the horse in their backyard in a barn. One morning John looked out the window and the barn door was open. John said, "Mom, the horse is on the loose." John was the youngest so no one believed him. They all looked out the window, but the horse was nowhere in sight.

"Come on kids we have to go look for Papoose—he is not here!" exclaimed Marilyn. "I will drive around town, and you children run through the neighborhood to see if you can catch Papoose."

Marilyn went speeding through the neighborhood. At the same time, Carole, Kathleen, Margaret, Thomas, and John ran through the neighbors' yards. As the children ran, Margaret collided into a clothesline and could not get untangled. "You guys keep going. I will go back and get Margaret off the Quinns' clothesline," yelled Thomas. Carole, Kathleen, and John kept on running to try to catch Papoose. When Margaret was freed, they took off as fast as their feet could carry them.

In the next yard, Thomas was not paying attention and tripped on a rock. Splat! In went Thomas in the fish pond. Everybody laughed except Margaret. Margaret went and helped Thomas out of the pond. She dried him off with some laundry that was on a clothesline, and they caught up with everyone else. They finally caught Papoose at the Ohmers' farm, where she had joined other horses. They walked Papoose home with its hooves going "click-clack click-clack." They were all very happy to have Papoose back.

The next morning, John looked outside, and the barn door was wide open. "Mom, the horse is gone again," John yelled impatiently. Their mother jumped in the car, and the children began their morning exercise of running to catch Papoose.

As they were running through the yard, Carole heard a dog bark and looked back. As she looked back, she ran into a rosebush. Thud! "Ouch!" yelled Carole. "That really hurts." Thomas helped Carole out of the rosebush and pulled the thorns out of her clothes. They quickly ran to catch up with the others.

A while later, John thought everyone was going too slow, so he ran in front of everyone else. As John looked back, he ran into a fence. The fence had wet paint all over it. Carole peeled John off the fence, and his clothes were covered in white paint. They ran so fast John was just a white blur.

When they finally caught Papoose, she was once again at the Ohmers' farm. They walked home with the horse's hooves going "click-clack, click-clack."

The next morning, John was afraid to look out the window for fear of what he would find. Sure enough...Papoose was on the loose. "Mom, Papoose is gone again!" screamed John. Their mom jumped in the car, and the children ran through the neighborhood. As they continued running through backyards, all of a sudden Kathleen heard a big dog bark. She turned her head to see how big the dog was and ran into a crab apple tree. Thud! Crash! Bang! All the crab apples came falling on Kathleen. Just as she thought things could not get any worse, all the crab apples had ants coming out of them. The ants crawled all over her body. "Yikes!" screamed Kathleen. Margaret was laughing because she always teased her with bugs.

Once again, they found Papoose at the Ohmers' farm. When they told the Ohmers about Papoose breaking loose, they all agreed that Papoose should live on the Ohmers' farm. The Kings visited Papoose often. Papoose never ran away again.

Teaching the Subgenre of Memoir

The general minilessons presented at the beginning of this chapter and the ARC strategy will help students understand the elements of memoirs. Comparing autobiographies to memoirs and narrowing the topic are also helpful as specific minilessons for teaching memoirs.

Comparing Autobiographies and Memoirs

An autobiography tells the life of the author. The author chooses the important events in his or her life that will be included in the autobiography. Because there are so many events that could be included, the author must decide on the theme or themes that constitute his or her life. Some events must be left out if they are not important to the theme. The framework of a complete autobiography is a lifeline, or a sequence of events from birth to the present.

A memoir, on the other hand, is not a review of a whole life, but a snippet of an event that has occurred during a person's life, told from that person's point of view. In *Inventing the Truth: The Art and Craft of Memoir* (1987) Zinsser writes, "Unlike autobiography, which moves in a dutiful line from birth to fame, omitting nothing significant, the writer of a memoir takes us back to a corner of his or her life that was unusually vivid or intense" (p. 21).

Calkins (1994) suggests that "memoir is not a life; it's a window into a life. It's a perspective on a life" (p. 406). The framework of a memoir is a sequence of feelings, thoughts, and observations about the event chosen.

Narrowing the Topic

Calkins (1994) writes that authors of both autobiographies and memoirs must narrow their topic. There must be a selection process. Authors of memoirs must select an event that is meaningful to their life. After the selection, there must come a personal reflection on this event: How does this event reflect my life? What feelings, thoughts, and observations are key to this event?

In her memoir, *When I Was Young in the Mountains* (1982), Rylant chooses only eight events or observations that add up to her one theme of how wonderful life was growing up in the mountains with a loving grandmother and grandfather. These events are quite mundane, but to Rylant, life in the mountains was wonderful in its simplicity:

> A kiss from Grandpa's clean lips
> A dinner of hot corn bread, pinto beans, and fried okra
> A trip to the johnny-house
> Swimming at the swimming hole
> Pumping pails of water for bathing
> Church services and baptisms
> Killing a snake and taking a photo of him draped over their shoulders
> Sitting on the porch at night

Reading the Memoir

Before the class read-aloud, share with students that a memoir is a retelling of a specific event or experience related to the author's life. Explain that as people live their lives, certain events or experiences happen, and they may want to share some of these experiences with others, so they write a memoir. Discuss how a memoir is different from a fictional story that an author may write. Explain that a memoir is written about a real-life experience of the author, whereas a fictional story is created from an author's imagination.

Select and read aloud a memoir to the entire class. The memoir that you select will depend on the age of your students. Fortunately, there are many excellent memoirs written for elementary age students. Although any memoir can be used for this activity (see Children's Literature Bibliography), the memoir *The Relatives Came* (Rylant, 1985) will be used in this section to illustrate teaching activities for a memoir. Other examples of memoirs include *Calling the Doves: El Canto de las Palomas* (Herrera, 1995), *Owl Moon* (Yolen, 1987), and *But I'll Be Back Again: An Album* (Rylant, 1989).

Share with students that the memoir *The Relatives Came* was written by Rylant to allow the reader to experience the summers that her relatives came to visit from Virginia. Following this discussion, read aloud the memoir to the entire class.

After the read-aloud, explain that when authors write a memoir, there are certain elements that they include in the text. The first element is an introduction, in which the author will share with the reader important information about the setting, including the time, date, or both of the experience. The information presented in the introduction usually answers who, what, where, when, and why. The completed graphic organizer in Figure 2 is an example of one used in the classroom as students follow the read-aloud. Students also can fill in Graphic Organizer: The Memoir (see Appendix A, page 93) as they read memoirs on their own.

Figure 2   Example of the Memoir Graphic Organizer

Introductory Statement:

Who	What	Where	When	Why
The relatives	came	from Virginia	in the summer	to visit

Sequence of Events:

1. Relatives left Virginia

2. They drove all day

3. They drank pop and ate crackers

4. They pulled into our yard

5. Hugging time began

6. Big supper was served

7. Quiet talk

8. Slept—breathing together

9. Tended the garden—fixed things

10. Headed back to Virginia

Closing Statement (optional):

"And when they were finally home in Virginia, they crawled into their silent, soft beds and dreamed about the next summer." (n.p.)

The introduction in the read-aloud book is found in the first line: "It was in the summer of the year when the relatives came. They came up from Virginia. They left when their grapes were nearly purple enough to pick, but not quite" (n.p.).

The next element of the memoir is a presentation of the details. In our read-aloud, we find events of the relatives' visit. As you read the book aloud, students can help generate a list of events, organize the events, and complete the graphic organizer.

The last element is the closing statement, which is optional in a memoir. Rylant does include a closing statement.

Writing the Memoir

The student writing of a memoir will follow the writing process. Calkins (1994) suggests helping students narrow their topic before writing by writing about one photograph that conveys the essence of their childhood. Students also could list events that they feel convey their life so far, then narrow their list to the most important event that matches the life theme they wish to convey to an audience. To begin the prewriting stage, ask students to browse through their writing notebooks or writing journals to identify a personal experience that they could share with others in a memoir. You may wish to share another read-aloud of a memoir before the students begin to generate topics for their memoirs.

You can model writing a memoir written about one of your life experiences. Once a topic is identified, students may fill in Graphic Organizer: The Memoir (see Appendix A, page 93) to begin to draft their memoir. Remind students to include their reflections, feelings, and observations of this experience.

The following memoir was written by Katie, a fourth grader:

Bullfrogs

It was a really hot and dry day when my friend, my brother, and I caught bullfrogs with our bare hands. We were at our Grandma's, and she has a pond in front of her house. So, after lunch, we rode our bikes down to the pond. We wanted to catch lots of bullfrogs and beat our record from last year. We don't usually get to go to the pond, because the little kids that Grandma sits with like to follow us around. But it was really hot outside, and all the little kids were in the house.

When we got down to the pond, we took off our shoes and started to catch bullfrogs with our bare hands. While we were catching frogs, we saw some fat leeches. My friend screamed, because they were gigantic!

She said, "I think they are going to be able to eat me!"

I said, "No they're not!"

She replied back, "Are too!"

"Are not!" I said again.

We argued back and forth. Finally she gave up, and said, "OK, you win." I couldn't believe the words that had just come out of her mouth, because I am usually the one who has to give up first.

After we saw the leeches, we pretended to have cannon ball leeches on our feet, but they were just piles of sloppy mud. Soon, my friend got disgusted, but I sort of liked it. This whole time my brother, Brady, was catching frogs. He slipped while diving for a frog and made what looked like a mud slide. Boy, oh boy, did I feel bad for him, because he was so wet and muddy.

We took the squishy frogs back to our bikes carrying them in our bare hands. We rode back up to the house. Holding on to the frogs and the handlebars of my bike at the same time really squished the frogs. I felt bad for the frogs, even though I was the one squishing them. Then Brady suggested, "Why don't we give the frogs a bath and play with them in the sandbox?" Well, that's what we did! After a while, they looked sort of dried out, so we took them back to the pond.

When we got back to Grandma's house, we were really filthy. Grandma said, "You guys are all dirty, so you can't sit on the furniture."

So, we decided to go outside and wash off with the hose. We got ourselves and our clothes clean, but we were still wet. Then Grandma told us to take our wet clothes off and she would put them in the dryer. Pretty soon I was standing there with nothing on but wet underpants. Grandma told me to go in the bathroom and take off my underwear, but all she had for me to put on were training pants from one of the little kids. I had to wear those uncomfortable and embarrassing pants!

Like they always say, "All's well that ends well." Now, looking back, I realize that my day wasn't so bad after all, because it ended with breaking our record catching bullfrogs. However, next time, I'm going to bring a bucket to catch the frogs with. That way I won't get so dirty and have to wear "baby training pants" again!

Summary

This chapter presented suggestions for teaching the reading and writing of recounts. Two recount genres were studied in depth—the biography and the memoir. The reading and writing of biographies gives students the opportunity to study the accurate and factual accomplishments of another person's life. The reading and writing of memoirs gives students a glimpse into a meaningful event of an author's life and an opportunity to share remembrances from their own lives. Minilessons taught focused on how authors bring the reader into their recount by writing strong and enticing leads and how authors keep the reader engaged by using powerful words. Other minilessons helped students understand how authors locate and use information when writing biographies and select snippets of their lives when writing memoirs. Chapter 2 focuses on reading and writing procedural texts that explain or instruct.

Chapter 2

Teaching Procedural Texts

Procedural texts are written to help readers follow a set of steps to achieve an intended purpose. Authors of procedural texts bring order and sometimes safety to readers' lives by presenting a workable set of directions. The purposes or goals of procedural text are many and diverse, such as showing patriotism, saving a life, or just having fun. Readers rely on authors of procedural texts to help them prepare our meals, treat a snakebite, conduct a science experiment, care for a pet, or play a game.

There are two major purposes for writing procedural texts: to explain or to instruct. Procedural texts that explain are written to make clear and understandable how to achieve an intended goal or to detail a process of how something is created or prepared, such as *recipes*. Using a recipe, we know the specific equipment needed, the exact amount of various ingredients to mix, and directions for mixing and preparing the dish. The author of a recipe explains how to make this dish so it can be served with pride.

Procedural text also includes *manuals* for how to operate something such as a telephone, a gas grill, or a DVD player. Manuals are written in technical language that includes concise directions and sometimes diagrams.

Procedural texts also can explain a process. They may explain how milk is turned into cheese, how metal is turned into money, or how wool is turned into fabric for clothing. Often photographs accompany the text.

Procedural texts that instruct or teach are written to guide or inform a reader. An example of a procedural text that instructs is *game rules*, which present instructions that ensure that a game is played the same way every time. The structure includes the number of participants, equipment needed, the objective of the game, and the rules of play. When readers finish reading game rules, they can play the game fairly.

Science experiments, another type of procedural text that instructs, include a hypothesis about the results to be expected from the experiment, equipment needed, procedures to follow, and results. Directions must be written sequentially and in a manner that is easy to understand and follow. Often illustrations and diagrams further explain the directions.

Types of procedural texts include the following:

Instruct	Explain
how to build something	how to prepare food
how to play a game	how to care for something
how to conduct an experiment	how to treat something
how to organize	how something is made
how to write speeches or reports	how to operate something
how to get somewhere	

This chapter will present in-depth lessons that illustrate the two purposes of procedural text. By introducing recipes to students in grades 2 and 3, you can provide students with an awareness of procedural text that explains a set of steps to achieve an intended goal. Students in grades 4–6 can gain an understanding of procedural text that instructs by examining game rules.

General Procedural Text Minilessons

The following minilessons are brief, focused lessons that teach strategies for reading and writing procedural texts. They can be used before or during the reading of most procedural texts.

Procedural Prompts

Procedural texts that instruct, explain, or describe a process use bullets, numbers, or time-related words to help the reader follow along. These time-related words could include the following: *first, last, then, before, next, after, while.* For example, in *Kids' Book of Soccer: Skills, Strategies, and the Rules of the Game* (Clark, 1997) the author uses bullets to explain the art of heading the ball:

> The Keys to Heading:
> • Keep your mouth shut (so you don't bite your tongue).
> • Keep your eyes looking up, and on the ball!
> • Aim for just above your eyes, at the top of your forehead.
> • Get your upper body into the motion.
> • Attack the ball with the top of your forehead. (p. 42)

In *The Kid's Guide to Social Action*, Lewis (1998) uses numbers to designate ways to raise funds:

FIVE WAYS TO FUNDRAISE

1. Sell something.

2. Sell your services.

3. Ask for donations or sponsorships.

4. Hold an event.

5. Apply for a grant. (pp. 65–66)

In the book *Totem Pole* (Hoyt-Goldsmith, 1990), the author uses time-related words to give directions that show how a carver creates a totem pole:

The first step in making a totem pole is to find a straight tree.

After the right tree is found and cut down, all the branches are removed with an axe and the bark is stripped from the outside of the log.

When the log is ready to be carved, my father makes a drawing of how the pole will look when it is finished.

Next he uses a stick of charcoal to make a drawing on the log itself. Then he stands up on the log to see how the figures and animals look. When he is satisfied with the drawing, he takes up his tools and begins to carve. (pp. 14–15)

Reading Diagrams, Pictures, and Labels

Sometimes the best way to represent information in nonfiction texts is by diagrams and pictures that have labels. Explain to students that pictures or diagrams can support the text, but they also can give additional information. This is particularly true when explaining intricate directions. In *Super Simple Origami* (Kneissler, 2001), the author uses diagrams to explain folding techniques. She begins with a basic form and builds from it (see Figure 3). Notice how the illustrations clarify the meaning of the text. Sometimes the text and pictures are equally important to the description of a process; this is called a photo essay.

Command Verbs in the Present Tense

Explain to students that a sentence can be one word in length as long as that one word is a verb. Verb tenses indicate *time* in grammar. Present tense means that the action takes place in the present time. Explain, also, that when the verb is a command, *you* is understood as the verb's subject. Ask students to collect a list of present-tense command verbs to be placed on a word wall. The following are some examples from a recipe, followed by directions for making origami.

Figure 3   Example of Diagrams in Procedural Text

Penguins, fancy-dressed in their tuxedoes, and a few chunks of white plastic foam, for ice, can turn the table at a children's party into an arctic landscape.

Starting point: basic form A

Valley folds in the dashed lines (**1**).

Fold point **A** to point **C**, unfold. In the crease just created, fold points **B** and **D**, lying inside on the right, outward to the left (**2**).

Valley folds at points **B** and **D** (**3**).

Mountain fold in the center crease (**4**).

Turn model. Pull point **B** to the right (see next illustration). Turn model, and repeat with point **D**, turn (**5**).

At point **A**, reverse fold inside (**6**).

Reverse fold inside at points **A** and **C** (**7**).

Form the beak by reverse folds inside and outside at point **A**. Valley folds at points **B** and **D**. Reverse fold inside at point **C** (**8**).

The finished model (**9**).

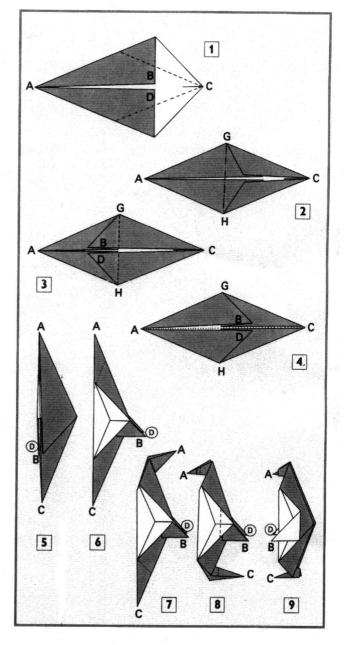

Kneissler, I. (2001). *Super simple origami.* New York: Sterling. Reprinted with permission.

Break 2 eggs into a small bowl. Beat them with a fork until they are completely yellow and smooth. Put a frying pan on the stove. Add 1 teaspoon oil, and then turn on the heat to medium. Wait for 30 seconds. (Katzen, 1999, p. 72)

Begin with your paper flat in a diamond shape. Fold it in half by bringing the top point to meet the bottom, and make a sharp crease. Fold the left and right points to the bottom point. (Smolinski, 2000, p. 12)

Detailed Information About Quantity and Quality: Time, Amount, Color, Size, Distance, and Range of Temperature

Giving concise, detailed information is crucial to procedural texts. Specific words denoting time, amount, color, size, distance, and range of temperature help the author communicate instructions explicitly. *The Little House Cookbook: Frontier Foods From Laura Ingalls Wilder's Classic Stories* (Walker, 1979) uses color, time, and range of temperature in the directions for fried fish: "Slice salt pork and fry to a crisp brown over medium heat, about 5 minutes to a side. Remove the crisp slices to a warm serving platter" (p. 45). In *100 Best Games* (Perez, 2000), the description of how to play "The Wall" uses amount and size or distance:

Two lines are marked in the middle of the playground, about five or six feet apart. This is the wall. Three players are chosen to be the taggers and stand on the wall. They can only move between the two lines. The rest of the players will stand on one side of the wall. (p. 89)

Building Background Knowledge for Procedural Texts

The PreReading Plan, or PReP (Langer, 1981, 1982), was developed to help students extend their understanding of a topic before reading. This strategy can be modified to help students extend their understanding of the purpose and structure of procedural texts.

Step one in PReP is the initial association with the genre. You might ask the question, "Tell me what comes to mind when you hear the word *recipes?*" (You may substitute any of the procedural genres.) Students might answer with words such as *directions, temperature, cookies, ingredients,* or *measurements.* You record their original responses on a chart, chalkboard, or dry-erase board.

Step two gives students the opportunity to evaluate and explore their responses to the question posed in step one. You could probe with questions such as, "What made you say *ingredients?*" Step three gives students the opportunity to add new ideas to their list. Students may add words such as *mix, sift,* or *time to cook.* PReP allows you to decide how much information students already know about the genre. At this time, you could pass out examples of the genre, in this case cookbooks, to continue their exploration of the genre. Students can then continue to add to the list, and you could add a step by placing the terms on a semantic map, such as the one that follows. Ask students to come up with the categories and fit the words from the list under each category.

Types of recipes	Words that tell what to do	Parts of a recipe
Main dishes	mix	ingredients
Vegetables	boil	oven temperature
Appetizers	spread	directions
Desserts	sift	measurements

Teaching the Subgenre of Recipes

The general minilessons presented at the beginning of this chapter and the PReP strategy will help students read and write recipes. Using a glossary and using an index are also helpful as specific minilessons for teaching about recipes.

Using a Glossary

Share with students that some authors include a glossary in their procedural books. Explain that a glossary is similar to a dictionary, but the words included in the glossary are only the words that the author used in the book. They are the more difficult or technical words, so an explanation is given. The following is an example of a glossary entry from *The Little House Cookbook* (Walker, 1979): "Crimp. As used here, to pinch the edge of pastry into a fixed wavy pattern, often sealing together top and bottom crusts. Crimping is usually done with the thumb and index finger" (p. 220).

Using an Index

Tell students that an author might include an index, in which page numbers for the important topics in the text are listed. The terms in the index are arranged alphabetically, which saves readers time, and the index is located at the back of the book. Explain that indexes are helpful because if readers want to locate a certain recipe or an ingredient for a recipe, they do not have to read the entire book to locate it.

Reading the Recipe

Suggest that you want to make a peanut-butter-and-jelly sandwich. Ask students what you need to know in order to make this sandwich (you need to know the ingredients and the directions for making this sandwich). Ask students to list the ingredients. Then ask students to give you directions for making this sandwich. What information is relevant and what information is not relevant? To build background knowledge about recipes, look with the students at some cookbooks written for adults and cookbooks that are written for students (see Children's Literature Bibliography for other titles of recipe books).

Graphic Organizer: The Recipe (see Appendix A, page 94) can be used to plot the recipe format from a cookbook for young readers. For example, using information in the recipe "The World's Best Peanut Butter" found in *Honest Pretzels and 64 Other Amazing Recipes for Cooks Ages 8 & Up* (Katzen, 1999, pp. 52–53), the completed graphic organizer would look like that in Figure 4.

Figure 4   Example of the Recipe Graphic Organizer

Title: The World's Best Peanut Butter
Yield: This recipe makes about one cup.
Time: It takes about 5 minutes to make, start to finish.

Ingredients:
- 1½ cups peanuts (raw or roasted)
- ¼ teaspoon salt (if the peanuts are unsalted)
- 1 tablespoon plus 1 teaspoon peanut oil or canola oil (Katzen, 1999, p. 52)

Equipment (optional):
- Measuring cups and spoons
- Blender or food processor fitted with the steel blade
- Dinner knife and/or a narrow rubber spatula for scraping the peanut butter out of the machine
- Jar or container with a lid

Procedure:
- Measure 1½ cups peanuts into food processor.
- If the peanuts are unsalted, add ¼ teaspoon salt.
- Turn on the machine. (Use the "chop" or "blend" speed if you're using a blender.)
- Keep running the machine for about two or three minutes, or until the peanuts begin to turn into mush.
- Stop the machine and add 1 tablespoon plus 1 teaspoon oil. Buzz the machine (press the button on and off) a few more times until the oil is mixed in.... Then scrape the rest of the peanut butter into a jar or container with a lid.
- Keep it in the refrigerator.
Time to eat! (p. 53)

Ask students to bring in family recipes to share with the class. Discuss the parts of their recipes. Do they fit the text features we have identified? Students can use the graphic organizer to plot the recipes they share with the class.

Writing the Recipe

Now that students are familiar with the organizational structure of a recipe, have them write recipes that they can share with the class. Remind students to break their procedure into easy-to-follow steps. To integrate the study of recipes in the elementary curriculum, ask students to write a recipe from a country the class is studying, a family recipe, or a recipe using a certain product the class is studying. The student writing of a recipe will follow the writing process. As a prewriting exercise, ask students to fill in Graphic Organizer: The Recipe (see Appendix A, page 94). The following recipe was written by Michael, a second grader:

Salsa

    1 cup tomatoes
    1 cup apples
    ⅔ cup sauce
    16 cups chilies
    ½ cup water

First, add 1 cup of cut-up tomatoes. Next, add ⅔ cup of sauce. Then add chopped up chilies. Fourth, add the water. Finally, add chopped up apples.

Teaching the Subgenre of Game Rules

The general minilessons presented at the beginning of the chapter and the PReP strategy will help students read and write game rules. Variations on original rules and using a table of contents are specific minilessons for teaching about game rules.

Variations on Original Rules

Explain to students that sometimes games can be played in a number of ways. Other times, if you have more than the optimum number of players, game rules change. In *100 Best Games* (Perez, 2000), the author explains the game of "Keep Away" and then tells a variation of this game:

> One of the teams passes the ball among its players while the players on the opposite team try to catch or intercept it. The team that catches the ball starts tossing it again.
>   When a player has the ball in his hands, he can only make a maximum of three passes.
>   *Variations:* The first team to pass the ball 10 times without dropping it or being intercepted wins. (p. 73)

In the book *Sidewalk Games Around the World*, Erlbach (1997) tells her audience what to do if they want to play the game "Four Square" with more players than the four initially recommended:

> Directions for more than 4 players: Instead of becoming the Dunce, the player who makes an out is out of the game. The remaining 3 players move up in rank, leaving an empty Dunce square, and a new player enters as Dunce. (p. 13)

Using a Table of Contents

Share with students that they can find out a lot about a book before reading it by looking at the table of contents. Included in the table of contents are titles and beginning page numbers of each chapter in the book. If a reader is looking for a specific topic, he or she can look in the table of contents instead of paging through the entire book to locate it. For example, in *Sidewalk Games Around the World* (1997), Erlbach uses the country names as categories to organize the table of contents.

Reading Game Rules

Share a written sample of rules for a game that is familiar to your students. The game rules that you share with the students will depend on the students' abilities and interests (see Children's Literature Bibliography for children's books containing game rules). The read-aloud book for this activity is *Games Around the World: Jacks* (Jaffe, 2002). Read pages 18 and 19 to the students. As you read, have the students fill in the Graphic Organizer: Game Rules (see Appendix A, page 95). Figure 5 shows an example of a filled-in graphic organizer for our read-aloud.

Writing Game Rules

Now that students are familiar with the organizational structure of game rules, have the students write out rules for a game they have played or a game they have invented. Students can use Graphic Organizer: Game Rules (see Appendix A, page 95) as they plan to write their game rules. After they have finished their first draft, ask students to present their game rules to a friend to see if the friend can follow the rules and understand the number of players, the materials or equipment needed to play, the goal of the game, and how to play the game. The rules can then be revised, edited, and published.

Figure 5　Example of the Game Rules Graphic Organizer

Title of Game: Jumpin' Jacks
Number of Players: One or more
Equipment (what we need): Ten jacks and a small rubber ball
Goal (object): To go from onesies to tensies and back down again

How to Play (rules of the game):
1. Scatter 10 jacks on the ground.
2. The first round is onesies. The first player must pick up all 10 jacks, one at a time. You can't miss or drop a jack. You must catch the ball after one bounce. Put each jack you pick up into the other hand, or set it aside.
3. After you have picked up all 10 jacks, scatter all the jacks again. Begin the next round—twosies.
4. If you don't make any mistakes, go on to the next round.
5. If you make a mistake, you are out. Then it is the next player's turn.
6. The first player to play up to tensies and back down to onesies wins! (Jaffe, 2002, pp. 18–19)

Variations:
1. Kong-Keui—South Korea (p. 20)
2. Osselets—Haiti (p. 24)

The following example of game rules was written by Ivy, Sam, and David, from grades 3 and 4:

Title of Game: Space Blast
Number of Players: 2–5
Equipment:
>   One space board (designed by student)
>   12 trivia cards
>   30 tokens
>   5 playing pieces
>   1 die

Goal: Try to get all the trivia questions right and collect the most tokens.
How to Play:
Set-up:
>   Take out board. Put board on flat surface. Take out 12 trivia cards. Pick playing piece. Put trivia cards face down on corner of the board.

Playing the game:
>   The first person to get a trivia question goes first. Play continues to the left.
>   Roll the die and then move as many spaces as the die says.

If the space is colored you get a trivia question. If the space is blank you sit there until your next turn. If you get the question right, you get a token. If you get it wrong, you sit there until your next turn.

How to win:
The first person to get all of the colored tokens or gets to the end first wins.

Summary

This chapter presented two purposes of procedural text, to explain and to instruct, and we have discussed the genres associated with these two purposes. We selected the genre of recipes as an example of procedural text that explains. We used game rules as an example of procedural text that instructs. By emphasizing authors' purpose and the text structures of the genres of procedural text, we designed mini-lessons about chronological order; diagrams, pictures, and labels; present-tense command verbs; quantity and quality in written language; and timesaving devices for readers such as indexes and tables of contents. Chapter 3 discusses sequentially ordered texts, which present information in a predictable structure.

Chapter 3

Teaching Sequentially Ordered Texts

Authors may use a variety of text types to present information. Some authors develop texts that use a predetermined pattern to present information sequentially. Readers can use the predictability of the structure to understand the information given. Examples of this type of text are alphabet (ABC) and counting books and cycle books.

ABC and *counting books* are informational books in which the author decides on a topic or theme and presents the details using letters of the alphabet or numbers to sequence the information. Many times, readers think of alphabet and counting books as designed for young children, but now there are many books that give a wealth of information on various topics appropriate for older readers. Other alphabetically ordered books include atlases, dictionaries, encyclopedias, indexes, and telephone directories.

Authors of *cycle books* organize or group ideas according to the order in which they occur in nature. The cycle of events begins and ends at the same point. For example, the life cycle of a butterfly begins and ends with the egg. The topics of cycle books are presented in recurring patterns, such as migration, the life cycle, or seasonal, monthly, or yearly cycles. Students seem to be attracted to cycle books at an early age because authors present the facts in an orderly and logical manner.

Subgenres of procedural text include the following:

ABC books	indexes
atlases	life cycles
calendars	number books
cycles of time	telephone directories
dictionaries	time lines
encyclopedias	

In this chapter, we will discuss teaching ABC informational books and cycle books. Students in grades 2 and 3 would enjoy creating an ABC or counting book about a topic they are studying. Students in grades 4–6 would relish the logic of the patterns laid out in the cycle books.

General Sequentially Ordered Text Minilessons

Minilessons are brief, focused lessons that teach strategies for reading and writing sequential text. They can be used before or during the reading of most sequentially ordered text.

Creating Word Pictures With Adjectives

The text of most ABC, counting, and cycle books is short, so the information presented must create pictures that expand the information in the readers' minds. Explain to or review with students the definition of adjectives, and discuss how adjectives create these word pictures. In *A Walk in the Rainforest* (1992), Pratt uses alliterative adjectives such as

> "a gentle giant Gorilla grinning in the green growth" (p. 13)
> "a ravishing Red-eyed Tree Frog with big, bulgy eyes" (p. 24)
> "a vibrant Vanilla Orchid with very flavorful fruit" (p. 28)

In the cycle book *Animal-Go-Round* (Morris, 1993), the author uses photographs and adjectives to describe each animal. Each animal's growth is presented in a wheel: "Spin the wheel to see this timid little baby grow into a big, bouncy rabbit. Here are tiny twin lambs. In one turn of the wheel, see a lamb grow into a fleecy sheep" (n.p.).

Beginning a Sentence With a Prepositional Phrase

Varying the way you begin sentences is important to keeping a reader's interest. Explain to or review with students the meaning of *prepositional phrase*, and give examples. In the examples that follow, the authors have used a prepositional phrase to add variety to their sentences and to show sequence:

> "As the caterpillar grows, it sheds its skin." (Legg, 1998, p. 14)
> "When the caterpillar is fully grown, it gets ready to turn into a butterfly." (Legg, 1998, p. 19)
> "After only three weeks, the young hummingbirds are almost full grown." (Himmelman, 2000, n.p.)

"On a sunny summer morning, one hummingbird flies off on his own." (Himmelman, 2000, n.p.)

"By staying in the tentacles, the Clownfish is safe from other fish who might eat it." (Pallotta, 1991, n.p.)

Highlighting Content Area Words

When authors want to present new words that are important to the subject, they often highlight these words in some way. In ABC books, these words are often the alphabetical words, which are then defined by the text. For example, this occurs in *A is for Asia* (Chin-Lee, 1997):

> **B is for batik, an Indonesian craft.** Batik designers create a picture in wax on a piece of cloth. They then dye the cloth in different colors. Each time they dye the cloth, they re-move the wax and apply it in different places, creating rich patterns, like these gold and orange ripples on a sea of blue. (n.p.)

In *The Sailor's Alphabet* (McCurdy, 1998), a sea chantey, the content area words are highlighted in the text, but also are defined at the bottom of each page:

> K is the keelson away down below....
> KEELSON: A longitudinal beam fastened above and parallel to the keel of a ship to add strength. (n.p.)

Sometimes instead of defining words within the text, authors define words in a glossary (see also chapter 2 for a minilesson on glossaries). In *A Hummingbird's Life*, Himmelman (2000) collects words that are important to the topic in a "Words You Know" list. Legg (1998) uses a similar device in *From Caterpillar to Butterfly* and calls the glossary "Butterfly Words." In addition, this author also uses labels on diagrams to show information.

Adding Excitement to a Text

Review punctuation with students, and mention that in many sequentially ordered books, an exclamation mark often follows an unusual fact or a lighthearted sentence. For example, in *A Hummingbird's Life* (Himmelman, 2000), the hungry hummingbird spies a bright pink flower. Unfortunately, it is a flower on the shirt of a young girl: "Along the way, the hungry hummingbird spots a bright, pretty flower. But it is not a real flower! The hummingbird flies away" (n.p.).

The Underwater Alphabet Book (Pallotta, 1991) is filled with surprises, such as,

> C is for Cowfish, Moo! Don't be silly. Cowfish do not moo, but some people think that they look like cows with horns. A Cowfish has bony plates on the outside of its body. You could say that this fish lives inside its own box! (n.p.)

Building Background Knowledge for Sequentially Ordered Texts

Students will be reading a variety of sequential texts. As they read, they will become aware of the different text structures that authors use to present information. To assess students' prior knowledge of sequential text structure, use freewriting prior to reading sequential texts (Elbow, 1973). Freewriting is writing that is unrestricted in form, style, content, and purpose; the goal is to get words onto paper. Elbow designed this technique to help students focus on content rather than mechanics, but this strategy works well to build the background about purpose and structure of sequential texts.

Share with students that they will be learning about the sequential text of cycles (or ABC or counting books, or dictionary or encyclopedia entries). Then, introduce the subgenre and ask the students to quickly write words or phrases that are associated with this type of book. Give students only four or five minutes to write. An example of a student's freewriting for cycle books might look like the following:

a chain	time-related words
ordered events	cycles
progression of events	diagrams
series	start to finish
naturally occurring events	facts

After the four to five minutes, ask students to share their responses. At this time, assess background knowledge of the subgenre by listening for correct and incorrect responses. Once the responses have been shared, read aloud a book that exemplifies the subgenre.

After this read-aloud, ask students to revisit their freewrite to revise their ideas by adding or subtracting words or phrases. As the unit progresses, students can continue to revise their freewrites.

Teaching the Subgenre of ABC Books

The previous general minilessons and the freewriting strategy will help students read and write ABC books. Using alliteration and using onomatopoeia also are helpful, specific lessons for teaching ABC books.

Using Alliteration

Share with students that if the author wants to write in a catchy and entertaining way, he or she may use the poetic device *alliteration*, or the repetition of the initial consonant sounds in words that are close to one another. Share some examples of alliteration and highlight the repetition of the initial consonants. For example, Pratt uses alliteration in the phrases in her book, *A Swim Through the Sea* (1994): "He could confront a crazy-colored Clownfish, or discover a dozen delightful Dolphins diving up and down" (n.p.).

Using Onomatopoeia

Explain that when an author wants to write so that the reader can "hear" the words, he or she may use another poetic device called *onomatopoeia*. Tell students that onomatopoeia is the use of sound words or words that imitate sounds. Wargin uses onomatopoeia in her ABC book *L is for Lincoln: An Illinois Alphabet* (2000). For example,

> Now N is for the Northern Cross,
> the first railroad in our state
> to be drawn by locomotive,
> it made transportation great!
> Chug, chug, move along.
> Chug, chug, fast and strong.
> T is for the Tully Monster—
> it was an animal in motion,
> swimming through the water
> when our state was just an ocean.
> Splish Splash. Gone in a flash! (n.p.)

Reading the ABC Book

Expose students to ABC books by beginning with a class read-aloud. Before the read-aloud, share with students that an ABC book can be created for just about any topic. Usually, the book is written about a topic that the author knows very well and wants to share in an interesting and fun way. The author links the facts about the topic to the letters of the alphabet, and the book is organized sequentially with the facts and ideas presented from A to Z.

To begin the study, select an ABC book to share with students. Although any alphabet book can be used (see Children's Literature Bibliography for titles of ABC books), in this section we will use *A Swim Through the Sea* (Pratt, 1994).

In some ABC books, the author gives the reader an overview of the topic in an introduction. Tell students that after this introduction, the author begins to present the facts or ideas sequentially, following the letters of the alphabet. Point out to students that Pratt uses alliteration as she weaves facts about the sea through the alphabet. She presents each alphabet letter in a phrase and continues on the next page with the next alphabet letter and another phrase. Her introduction sets the stage by introducing a seahorse that explores the sea and by describing what this seahorse will see.

As you read the pages of this book, ask students to fill in Graphic Organizer: The ABC Book (see Appendix A, page 96), which will look similar to the completed example in Figure 6. Point out to students that on the page containing the phrase for *A*, the author includes a descriptive paragraph about the attributes of angelfish. In the descriptive paragraph, Pratt describes how angelfish got their name, where they live, what they do during the day and at night, their size, how they eat, and if they mate for life. She continues this descriptive text structure through the end of the alphabet. Pratt has chosen to include a conclusion to the readers' alphabet journey through the sea.

Figure 6   Example of the ABC Book Graphic Organizer

Title: *A Swim Through the Sea*

Introduction to Topic (optional):
If Seamore the seahorse, who lives beneath the sea, one day went exploring, what do you think he'd see?

A—word, phrase, or sentence with A:
He'd admire an amiable
Angelfish in appealing apparel,

Descriptive sentence or paragraph:
Angelfish are named for their wide, wing-like fins. Among the many colorful species, the queen angelfish, like this one, are by far the most spectacular.

B—word, phrase, or sentence for B:
and bump into bright Blue Crabs.

Descriptive sentence or paragraph:
Blue crabs are three to nine inches wide with an olive-colored oval shell, or carapace.

Conclusion (optional):
So, swimming back home on a bright sunny day, Seamore the seahorse would certainly say: "I'm amazed at the beauty I've seen on the way, and surely expect that's the way it will stay. But it's going to take you, and it's going to take me, to keep it a beautiful, colorful sea." (n.p.)

To demonstrate that ABC books often follow similar formats, share the ABC book *Baseball ABC* (Mayers, 1994), and point out that this author uses different fonts for the letters of the alphabet and photographs to illustrate the words for the alphabet letters she is using. Mayers begins with the following introduction:

> This ABC is for baseball fans of all ages. In these pages you'll find photographs that capture the thrill of America's national game; you'll meet some of baseball's greatest players; and you'll see team pennants, caps, and jerseys, both old and new. From A for autograph to K for knuckleball to T for ticket and trophy, each letter gives you a bit of vital information about baseball history, tradition, or equipment. (n.p.)

She then begins with the letter A and gives some descriptive sentences:

> A—autograph
> Babe Ruth was the first of twenty players to sign this page of the American All-Star Tour of Japan photo album in 1934.
> World Champions in 1950, the New York Yankees autographed this baseball.
> Ted Williams wrote his name across the sweet spot of this ball in 1955, when he hit .356. With a .406 batting average in 1941, Williams was the last player to hit over .400. (n.p.)

Mayers does not include a conclusion.

Writing ABC Books

Student writing of ABC books will follow the writing process. Students can use Graphic Organizer: The ABC Book (see Appendix A, page 96) as a prewriting exercise. The writing of an ABC book may be incorporated into any unit of study and can be a whole-class project. You can introduce the idea of writing an ABC book for a specific topic at the beginning of the unit of study, and as the unit proceeds, students can collect ideas for their books. Students may volunteer to research individual letters and begin to draft their ideas and their descriptive sentences or paragraphs. Invite students to include photographs, illustrations, or both for each letter.

The following examples were written by students in a combined grade 2–3 classroom, Alex and Hannah, respectively:

P is for Penguin
Penguins live on the arctic tundra.
They get their water from the snow.
They eat fish, squid, krill and crab.
Penguins use snow banks and snowdrifts for shelter.

C is for Coyote
Coyotes live in deserts and forests.
They get their water from ponds.
They eat mice, dead animals, fish, birds, and garbage.
They get their shelter from dens.

Teaching the Subgenre of Cycle Books

The general minilessons and the freewriting strategy will help students read and write cycle books. Using labels in diagrams and using present-tense verbs are also helpful, specific lessons for teaching cycle books.

Writing Labels With Diagrams

Tell students that some authors create diagrams that use both words and pictures to give facts. Labels explain what the picture is showing. To help students understand how to write labels, give them a group of pictures for a cycle they are studying and have them write the labels. The labels should be short descriptions of the diagram. Use the diagram in Figure 7, which has been reprinted from the book *From Caterpillar to Butterfly* (Legg, 1998), as an example.

Using Present-Tense Verbs

Explain to students that authors use present-tense verbs to describe the action in a cycle book to show that the action is not something that took place only once in the past. Instead, the action in a cycle book occurs over and over now, in the present. For example, from *A Hummingbird's Life* (Himmelman, 2000): "As the hummingbird makes his journey, he stops for a snack. The hummingbird gets stuck in a garden spider's web" (n.p.). The present tense also is used throughout the cycle book *From Caterpillar to Butterfly* (Legg, 1998):

> When the caterpillar is fully grown, it gets ready to turn into a butterfly. It hangs down on a silk thread from a leaf stem. Then it sheds its skin for the last time to form a pupa. Inside the pupa, the caterpillar changes into a butterfly. (p. 19)

Figure 7   Example of Diagram With Labels

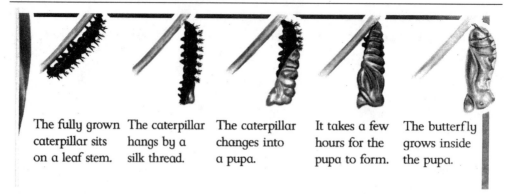

The fully grown caterpillar sits on a leaf stem. The caterpillar hangs by a silk thread. The caterpillar changes into a pupa. It takes a few hours for the pupa to form. The butterfly grows inside the pupa.

From *From Caterpillar to Butterfly* by Gerald Legg, illustrated by Carolyn Scrace, ©1998 Children's Press/Franklin Watts, a division of Scholastic, Inc. Reprinted with permission.

Reading Cycle Books

Before the class read-aloud, share with students that a cycle book is an account of something that begins and ends at a point in time. The author describes the aspects of this event sequentially, explaining what happens first, second, third and continues to the end of the cycle, which is when the cycle begins again.

Select and read aloud a cycle book to the class. The cycle book you select will depend on your students and the topics you are studying in the classroom. Therefore, any cycle book can be used that complements the curriculum (see Children's Literature Bibliography for more titles of cycle books). Here we will discuss the book *A Hummingbird's Life* (Himmelman, 2000). While you read the book aloud, ask students to fill in Graphic Organizer: The Cycle Book (see Appendix A, page 97). Figure 8 shows an example of a filled-in graphic organizer for the read-aloud. The cycle can be shown in a circle format.

Figure 8   Example of the Cycle Book Graphic Organizer

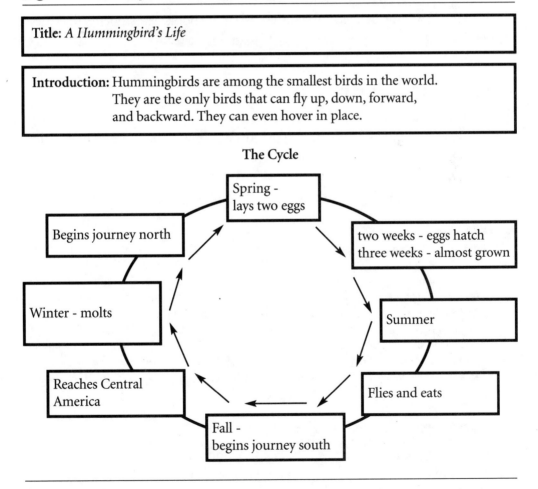

Title: *A Hummingbird's Life*

Introduction: Hummingbirds are among the smallest birds in the world. They are the only birds that can fly up, down, forward, and backward. They can even hover in place.

The Cycle

Spring - lays two eggs

two weeks - eggs hatch
three weeks - almost grown

Summer

Flies and eats

Fall - begins journey south

Reaches Central America

Winter - molts

Begins journey north

During the read-aloud, explain that authors of cycle books include an introduction to their topic at the beginning of the book. What follows is Himmelman's introduction:

> Ruby-throated Hummingbird
> *Archilochus colubris*
> Hummingbirds are among the smallest birds in the world. They are the only birds that can fly up, down, forward, and backward. They can even hover in place. (n.p.)

The author continues the introduction with more about this hummingbird—where it lives, what it looks like, and migration patterns.

Next, the author describes the life cycle of the hummingbird by sharing the bird's yearly calendar, starting with the laying of two eggs: "In spring, a female ruby-throated hummingbird lays two eggs. Two weeks later, young birds *hatch* from the eggs. After only three weeks, the young hummingbirds are almost full grown" (n.p.). The text continues through the year's events and ends with the hummingbird flying north in the spring to lay two eggs, and the cycle begins again. Himmelman has italicized words that will appear in a glossary at the end of the book. Tell students that these are the words the author feels should be defined for the reader.

Writing Cycle Books

The writing of a cycle book will follow the writing process. Students can use Graphic Organizer: The Cycle Book (see Appendix A, page 97) as a prewriting exercise. Writing a cycle book can be incorporated into any unit of study in which cycles are discussed.

The student example that follows was written by Zachery, grade 5:

The Facts About Salmon: Life Cycle

Salmon have a long life cycle. In the first stage of a fish's life, they go through a period of being eggs. Salmon eggs lay in a "nest" that is called a redd. The salmon lays about 3,000–7,000 eggs. Then in the second stage, they hatch and start to eat their yolk sac. The sac contains protein, sugar, minerals, and vitamins…but as these alevins grow the sac disappears. In the third stage, they are fingerlings. They have gone past the stage of being the size of pine-needles.

The last stage is when they are three years old. In the adult stage, they weigh up to 80 pounds. The salmon have a better chance of getting attacked so they swim away. Then they go back and lay their eggs. After they lay their eggs, they start to swim up the river. At this time in their lives, they are as red as cherries on a tree. As they swim, their bodies disintegrate. They fall apart and die.

Summary

In this chapter, we have discussed the reading and writing of books that are sequentially organized by the author. Students have been exposed to text structures that help them understand and remember the information presented. We have discussed ways in which authors create word pictures by using descriptive adjectives and poetic language, how authors incorporate different sentence structures using prepositional phrases, and methods authors use to define scientific and technical terms. Graphic organizers were shared for student reading and writing of sequentially ordered texts. In the next chapter, we continue our discussion of nonfiction texts by introducing informational books that lead students to the writing of reports and to the reading and writing of travel brochures.

Chapter 4

Teaching Informational Texts

Information seeking is a common activity for readers of any age, whether the purpose is to find new information on a topic of interest or to confirm information that is already known. For our discussion in this chapter, informational text is nonfiction writing that has the main purpose of presenting factual information on a specific topic or event.

Informational text is the most complicated type of nonfiction text because the purposes for writing this genre are so varied. The purpose of informational text, as with the other types of nonfiction genres, dictates the structure. The purposes for reading informational texts include the following: to obtain a detailed description, to define the topic, to identify causes and effects of certain things related to the topic, to identify how one thing differs from another, to present information related to the topic sequentially, or to find out about the problems associated with the topic and find solutions to these problems. Because there are so many purposes and text structures directly tied to text purpose, not all informational texts have the same text structures. Subgenres of informational texts include the following:

announcements	descriptions
book jackets	diagrams
book reports	documents
brochures	explanations
catalogs	guidebooks
cereal boxes	historical plaques
charts	interviews
constitutions	introductions
contracts	lab reports
definitions	lists

maps	question-and-answer books
menus	questionnaires
problem/solution books	reports
	weather reports

The subgenres explored in depth in this section are types of informational texts that elementary students can explore by both reading and writing. *Informational books* and the corresponding student *reports* are factual pieces of writing that present information in an organized and clear fashion. The text organization of an informational book or report is content-specific and relates to the purposes the author wants to achieve. For example, in the book *Fishes* (Stewart, 2001), the author uses both description and problem/solution text structures in the following paragraph:

> Most fish eggs are no bigger than the head of a pin. They may drift in the water, sink to the bottom, or stick to plants or rocks. Many are eaten by other fishes. To make sure that enough young fish will develop, a female fish may lay hundreds of eggs at a time. A female cod may lay more than 8 million eggs a year. (pp. 37–38)

A *travel brochure* is a document that describes a place and includes its attributes. This type of writing is generally descriptive. The *travel postcard* is a short informational text that tells others about a place visited, usually with a picture on one side. A *guidebook* is a text that contains directions or descriptions of places for travelers to see or categories of objects such as birds, plants, and shells to identify.

Another type of informational book is the *question-and-answer book*. In this book, the author poses questions with the answers immediately following. Question-and-answer books usually are organized around a specific topic, such as sharks, the Underground Railroad, or dinosaurs.

In this chapter, we will discuss teaching reports and travel brochures. Students in grades 3–6 can explore reports, and students in grades 4–6 can design travel brochures.

General Informational Text Minilessons

The following minilessons are brief, focused lessons that teach strategies for reading and writing informational text. They can be used before or during the reading of most informational texts.

Using Present Tense and Subject-Verb Agreement

Many informational texts are written in the present tense. This will be easy for students to grasp. More difficult is the agreement of the present-tense verbs with their subjects. Subjects can be either nouns or pronouns. Review with students these terms and this relationship and provide examples. The book *Bison* (Winner, 2001), for example, uses nouns and pronouns as subjects and can be used to demonstrate how the author must be careful to have the correct subject-verb agreement. The boldface text in the following excerpt shows this agreement:

> **Bison use** their horns in several ways. Sometimes **two bison "lock** horns" and **push** each other back and forth, in a kind of shoving match to see which **one is** stronger. At other times **a bison sweeps** its head back and forth, using its horns to slash at the belly of its opponent. (p. 13)

Another example can be found in Kalman and Everts's book *Frogs & Toads* (1994): "**Frogs and toads sleep**, or **hibernate**, through the winter. **A frog dives** down to the bottom of a pond and **buries itself** in mud" (p. 22).

Using Similes

As discussed in chapter 3, when trying to describe a subject to the reader, adjectives can be very useful. Another technique authors use is to describe the unknown by comparing it to a known using *similes*. Explain to students that a simile uses the words *like* or *as* in an indirect comparison. Authors may choose to use a simile to describe something more quickly than writing a long description. Examples of similes used as comparisons are found in *Rain Forest Babies* (Darling, 1996):

> Lemurs didn't invent piggyback rides, but the babies sure like them. Little ring tailed lemurs ride like jockeys. Brown lemur babies wrap around their mother's waist like a belt. (n.p.)
>
> Big iguanas...look like something from a horror movie. (n.p.)

Two other examples can be found in *Frogs & Toads* (Kalman & Everts, 1994) when the authors describe frogs' and toads' eyes. The adjectives *beautiful* and *brilliant* are enhanced by these similes: "Some frogs and toads have beautiful eyes that come in brilliant colors. Some eyes look like gold or silver. Others look like jewels of red, blue, or green" (p. 18).

Forming Paragraphs

Share with students that a paragraph is a section of a piece of writing centered on a certain topic. Each paragraph is set off from the other paragraphs by indenting the first line. Although you need to teach the formation of a paragraph as a bundle of information about the same topic that has a topic sentence and detail sentences, this tidy definition is difficult to find practiced by authors. Many informational books have interesting formats that break apart paragraphs and wind them around illustrations and photographs, or the author may not indent the first paragraph on a page. The following two books have paragraphs that can be used as models for paragraph building. The authors of *Frogs & Toads* (Kalman & Everts, 1994) have included simple paragraphs: "Frogs and toads are cold blooded. They can die of heat during hot weather. They can freeze to death in cold weather. In the winter, frogs and toads must find warm homes to stay alive" (p. 22). In *Bison* (Winner, 2001), the author uses more complex paragraphs:

> Sometimes bison ignore a passing intruder such as a wolf or mountain lion. Other times, if the intruder seems ready to attack, they will challenge it. The bison paw the ground with their front hooves. They move closer, lowering their heads so their horns point forward. This warning is often all it takes to make the intruder back down and leave the area. But bison will fight if necessary, to protect themselves and the herd. (p. 27)

Building Background Knowledge for Informational Texts

Sampson, Sampson, and Linek (1994–1995) developed the Circle of Questions strategy to allow students to brainstorm and organize information prior to reading. Have students get into small groups. Announce the topic and give the student groups a period of time to brainstorm questions about the topic. After this time is up, draw a circle on the board, and write students' questions around the circle. Students help to put these questions into categories. Colored chalk is used to identify questions within the same categories. Each group then chooses a category to research. The students write the information and the source of the information by their questions. Figure 9 shows an example of a Circle of Questions (Sampson, Sampson, & Linek, p. 364).

Through Circle of Questions, students can see how authors of informational texts begin with questions and organize the answers to these questions into categories. These categories can be formed into headings or subheadings throughout the text. For example, if an author wanted to write an informational book about the Gulf of Mexico, he or she might brainstorm questions based on the purposes of informational books discussed earlier in this chapter. The questions that the author might brainstorm could include the following:

What is the Gulf of Mexico and where is it located? (definition)

What does the Gulf of Mexico look like? (description)

How does a gulf compare with an ocean? (compare-contrast)

What happens when storms hit? (problem/solution)

What is the history of the land area around the Gulf? (sequential/timeline)

What are the effects of pollution? (cause/effect)

Figure 9   Example of Circle of Questions Diagram

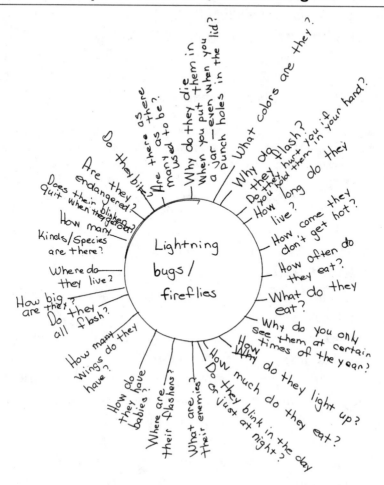

The circle contains: "Lightning bugs / fireflies"

Questions radiating from the circle:
- Do they bite?
- Are there as many as there used to be?
- Are they endangered?
- Does their light quit when they die?
- How many kinds/species are there?
- Where do they live?
- How big are they?
- Do they all flash?
- How many wings do they have?
- How do they have babies?
- Where are their flashers?
- What are their enemies?
- Do they blink in the day or just at night?
- How much do they eat?
- Why do they light up?
- How many times a day?
- Why do you only see them at certain times of the year?
- What do they eat?
- How often do they eat?
- How come they don't get hot?
- How long do they live?
- Do you hold them in your hand?
- Do they hurt you if you if
- Why do they flash?
- What colors are they?
- Why do they die when you put them in a jar even when you punch holes in the lid?

If the author wanted to write a guidebook about the Gulf of Mexico, the questions brainstormed might relate to the purpose of describing the sea creatures in the Gulf of Mexico:

What are plankton?

What mollusks live in the Gulf?

What crustaceans live in the area?

What fish live in the Gulf?

Do dolphins, whales, and manatees swim in the Gulf?

If the author wanted to write a travel brochure about the Gulf of Mexico, the questions would describe places to visit and directions for getting there:

What are the important Gulf coast towns?

What towns could tourists visit in the United States?

What could tourists see and do in Houston, Texas, USA? New Orleans, Louisiana, USA? Mobile, Alabama, USA? Pensacola, Florida, USA?

What towns could tourists visit in Mexico?

What could tourists see and do in Vera Cruz, Mexico?

What could tourists see in Havana, Cuba?

Teaching the Subgenre of Reports

The general minilessons and the Circle of Questions strategy will help students read and write reports. Using the specific lessons about the function of headings; about scan, skim, and read; about taking brief notes; and about using a variety of sentence beginnings will help students read and write reports.

The Function of Headings

An author's use of headings and questions offers a way to organize information. When writing, students can decide on their questions within a category, and these questions can be used as their headings. Sometimes authors may use questions to organize their book. In her book *Why Is Soap So Slippery? And Other Bathtime Questions*, Ripley (1995) includes the following questions as headings:

How can hot and cold water run out of the same tap?

Why do I have to brush my teeth?

Why do my fingers get so wrinkled in the tub?

Why can I draw on a mirror?

In *Frogs & Toads*, Kalman and Everts (1994) have included both statements and questions as headings:

In and out of water

What is a frog?

What is a toad?

Frog and toad homes

Authors who use headings probably began with some questions in mind. Have students look at headings and turn them into questions the author might have used to guide his or her research and writing. Petersen's book *The Gulf of Mexico* (2001) can be used as an example:

Paradise, Pirates, and Ports

Oceans, Seas, and Gulfs

The Gulf Stream

Under All That Water

Scan, Skim, and Read

Because not all reading is done at the same speed, Sloan and Latham (1988) developed the strategy of scan, skim, and read. You should model this strategy for your students. First, when looking for specific information, students should scan the text for headings, illustrations and captions, graphs, and vocabulary words that match their research focus. Then, students skim the information under those headings or near the illustrations and figures to see if it relates to their focus. Finally, if it is important, they read carefully while making notes.

Taking Brief Notes

When students begin the note-taking phase while reading informational books or preparing to write a report, a minilesson on the importance of not copying directly from the text will be useful. Also useful would be a discussion of the technique of writing on cards short, concise notes instead of writing complete sentences. Show students how to write their question or heading on the card along with the book title, author, date, and publication information. Emphasize that this information is important because students need to include a bibliography in their reports, as well (for discussion and a minilesson about bibliographies, see chapter 1). For instance, if a student chooses to read *What Is an Amphibian?* (Kalman & Langille, 2000) to research amphibians and how they reproduce, the student's brief notes on a card might look like this:

How do amphibians reproduce?

What Is an Amphibian?
By Bobbie Kalman and Jaqueline Langille
New York, Crabtree Publishing, 2000

Jelly coated eggs

Clutch—batch of eggs

Protect the eggs

After collecting all the information, the student can use these notes to write his or her own sentences:

How do amphibians reproduce?

Amphibians reproduce by laying soft, jelly coated eggs. They lay a lot of eggs. The batch of eggs is called a clutch. The amphibians protect their eggs.

Using a Variety of Sentence Beginnings

Students often begin each paragraph in the same way. Conversely, authors of informational books make sure to keep readers' interest by varying their paragraphs' topic sentences and detail sentences. The following are the topic sentences of three paragraphs used in the book *Bison* (Winner, 2001, p. 21):

"In their wandering, bison usually do not go to the same places every year."

"Bison move around so much to find food."

"The whole herd may move 10 to 15 miles (16 to 24 kilometers) in a day."

Looking at one of these paragraphs, students will note that the author has begun each of the sentences within the paragraph in a different way. For example,

Bison move around so much to find food. They are called herbivores (HERB-uh-vorz) because they eat only plants, mostly grass. On the plains it may look as if the grass never ends. So why would bison have to go looking for more food? If bison lived alone, they wouldn't have to travel as much. But they live in herds. And when thousands of bison come to an area, they quickly eat and trample the grass. Then they have to move on, to find more food. (p. 21)

Reading a Book for Information

As discussed earlier, informational texts are organized according to what the author wants to communicate about the topic, and the information is usually organized into paragraphs. When reading informational text, students can ask,

Does the author define the subject?

Does the author describe the subject? How?

Does the author compare the subject with something else?

Does the author show problems and solutions?

Does the author share what is happening or what has happened to the subject and discuss the effects?

Does the author present information sequentially about the subject?

Does the author use cue words to signal the text structure?

These same questions can be modified when students begin writing (see Graphic Organizer: The Report, Appendix A, page 98).

Bison (Winner, 2001), the book selected for the read-aloud in this section, will introduce students to informational text. Share with students that when authors introduce a topic, they usually will provide a definition of the subject for the reader. Winner shares several definitions throughout her book. Share the questions from the previous paragraph, and ask students to fill in the boxes in Graphic Organizer: The Report (see Appendix A, page 98) as you read aloud. Figure 10 shows an example of the graphic organizer completed with information found in *Bison*. However, you can use any informational book in this section. (See Children's Literature Bibliography for other informational book titles.)

As previously noted, the second purpose that can be served in informational writing is to define the topic. Descriptive writing is used to give details about the topic's attributes and features. Usually in descriptive writing, the author introduces the main topic and then includes the attributes in the body of the paragraph. Cue words associated with descriptive text include *first*, *second*, and *most importantly*. If many attributes are shared, the author may use a paragraph to discuss each attribute. Also, the focus of the information included in a descriptive paragraph may be sensory, or related to hearing, smelling, tasting, touching, and seeing. Questions to answer in the section of the graphic organizer that deals with descriptive text might include

Does the author describe the subject?

What is being described?

What did we learn about the topic?

Winner uses descriptive writing in *Bison* to tell readers about newborn bison, as well as the eating habits, travel patterns, and appearance of bison. Students can fill in the information from the read-aloud in the description section in the graphic organizer (see Figure 10 for an example).

Comparison text shows how two or more things are alike or different. Authors discuss the attributes of the items being compared to illustrate their differences and similarities. Cue words and phrases that signal this type of text include *but*, *however*, *although*, *similarly*, *on the other hand*, *while*, and *for instance*. Questions that can be asked about comparison text include

Does the author compare the subject with something else?

How are these items alike?

How are these items different?

Figure 10   Example of the Report Graphic Organizer

Title: Bison

Definition: They belong to the bovine (BO-vine) family, along with cattle, sheep, and goats. All of these species (SPEE-sees), or kinds of animals have horns, feet with two toes, and a stomach with four chambers. (p. 7)

Description: A newborn bison looks different from its parents. Its fur is reddish and it does not have a shoulder hump. It weighs between 30 and 70 pounds (13.6 to 31.8 kilograms) and is quite strong. (p. 39)

Other descriptions included by author:

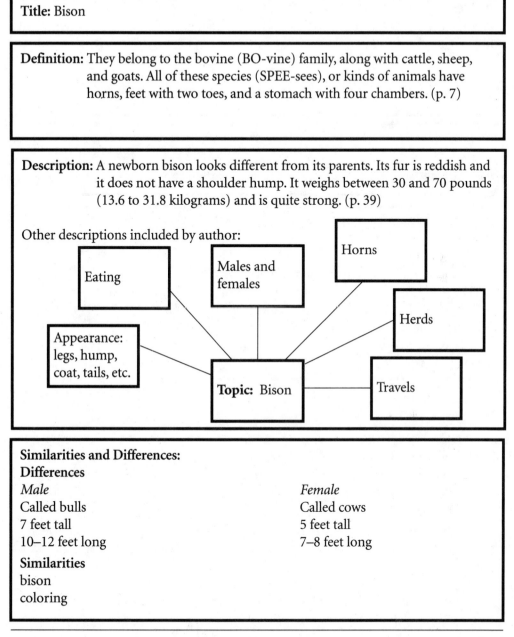

Similarities and Differences:
Differences
Male   *Female*
Called bulls   Called cows
7 feet tall   5 feet tall
10–12 feet long   7–8 feet long
Similarities
bison
coloring

continued

In the following excerpt, Winner (2001) describes the similarities and differences between the female and male bison. Note that in this excerpt, however, Winner does not use specific comparison cue words, so readers must ask questions as they read to identify similarities and differences between male and female bison:

Figure 10   Example of the Report Graphic Organizer (continued)

Problems and Solutions:

Problems	Solutions
Bison is attacked	Use horns to slash predator
Predators attack bison	Very good runners
Insect	Use tails to shoo away
Small calf may wander	Bulls stand guard

Cause and Effect:

Cause	Effect
Bison are startled	stampede

Sequence of Events:
Eating
1. Bison may graze for an hour or more.
2. Then they find a comfortable spot and lie down.
3. They bring up a previously swallowed wad of grass (cud) and chew it again.
4. They swallow that cud, bring up another, and chew some more.
5. Meal is finished.
6. Food passes to other chambers in the stomach.
7. Digestion continues.

Male bison are called bulls. They may stand up to 7 feet (2.1 meters) high at the shoulder. They are 10 to 12 feet (3 to 3.6 meters) long from the tip of their nose to their rump, and they weigh up to 1 ton (2,000 pounds or 909 kilograms). That's bigger than some sports cars! (p. 10)

Female bison are called cows. They are a bit smaller than bulls, standing about 5 feet (1.5 meters) tall at the shoulder. They measure 7 to 8 feet (2.1 to 2.4 meters) long, and they weigh about 800 pounds (364 kilograms). (p. 10)

During the read-aloud, students can fill in the differences and similarities sections of the graphic organizer as they explore how authors include differences and similarities between two items (see Figure 10 for example).

Problem/solution and cause/effect paragraphs are used to discuss causes and effects or to present problems and their solutions. Authors use problem/solution to present a problem, then include the possible solutions to this problem. Heller (1995) states, "When analyzing a topic, the author or reader examines the relationships between the parts and the whole in order to communicate or comprehend the structure of the underlying ideas" (p. 152). Cue words and phrases that signal problem/solution text include *the question is, the problem is, therefore, if,* and *then.* Questions that can be used to discover problem/solution relationships include the following:

What is the problem?

Is there a solution to the problem?

Does the author show problems and solutions?

The following examples from *Bison* (Winner, 2001) demonstrate problem/solution statements:

"If a predator, or enemy, such as a grizzly bear attacks a bison, the bison might slash it." (p. 13)

"But in order to attack a bison, predators have to catch up with it first. And that isn't easy, because bison are very good runners." (p. 15)

"Bison use their tails like whips to shoo the insects away, but they still get bitten, and that makes them itch even more." (p. 17)

Ask students to fill in the problem/solution section in the graphic organizer (see Figure 10).

Cue words and phrases that signal cause/effect text include *because, therefore, if…then, thus,* and *hence.* Questions that can be used to discover cause/effect relationships include the following:

What happened?

What were the reasons for this? What caused this to happen?

Does the author share what is happening to this topic and discuss the effects?

The following example from *Bison* (Winner, 2001) demonstrates how an author writes a cause/effect paragraph: "If bison are startled by a sudden danger such as fire or a loud storm, they often stampede (stam-PEED). In a stampede, the whole herd races off at a full gallop" (p. 28). Ask students to fill in the cause/effect section of the graphic organizer as they hear examples during the read-aloud (see, for example, Figure 10).

Finally, sequential text is used if the author wishes to inform readers about a topic by presenting information in lists, events, or steps in a sequence or in chronological order using time-related words. Cue words associated with this text type include *first, next, before, second, finally, then, when,* and *after.* Questions that can be asked to locate sequential text include the following:

Does the author present information in a sequential way?

What happened first, second, and third?

How were items in this paragraph organized: by age, time, etc?

Following is an example of sequential text describing how bison digest their food:

> Bison may graze for an hour or more at a time. Then they find a comfortable spot where they can lie down and rest. They bring up a wad of grass they swallowed earlier, called their cud, and chew it again. They swallow that mouthful, bring up another wad, and chew some more. Finally the meal is finished. It then passes to other chambers of the stomach, where digestion continues. (Winner, 2001, p. 26)

Ask students to fill in the sequence section of the graphic organizer to chart the sequence presented while you read aloud (see Figure 10 for an example).

Writing the Report

Now that students are familiar with how authors organize an informational book, students should be ready to write a report that is organized in the same manner. Writing the report will follow the writing process. Ask students to select a topic, then brainstorm questions and begin to research their topic. They can find information in the types of books discussed in this chapter, as well as in magazine and newspaper articles, encyclopedias, almanacs, and on the Internet. Students can then use the information gathered to begin prewriting. Pose questions such as the following for students to answer before they begin to write:

Do I need a definition in my report?

Do I want to provide a description for the readers?

Do I want to compare this item with another item?

Do I want to show problems and solutions?

Do I want to talk about what has happened to this topic and include the effects?

Do I want to write about a sequence of events related to my subject?

Students can decide how to answer these questions, then fill in Graphic Organizer: The Report (see Appendix A, page 98).

Finished reports and research projects can be published on the Web. For example, one second-grade teacher, along with her students, designed a website that included the informational book used, the research questions generated from the book, and the class report. Examples of classroom projects can be found on the Family Education Network's MySchoolOnline.com website (available http://www.myschoolonline.com).

The student writing sample that follows was written by Ashley, a fifth-grade student:

All About Moose
In the following report, you will hear about where moose live, what moose eat, what their sizes are, who their enemies are, even what a moose looks like if you happen to run into one.

Habitat
Where do Moose live? Well the Great North woods, of course, which ranges from Alaska through Canada until Maine and even in Europe and Asia. Moose spend their days eating, raising their young, protecting their young from all their enemies. During winter, moose do not hibernate, they stay living where they live in spring.

To run into a moose
If you were to see a moose, you would mostly find them in the north woods. They would look very large, fierce and mean…if you mess with their young or invade their territory, they will charge and stomp on you. Both male and female moose are light brown. The average height of the male is 6 feet tall. How to tell if you are looking at a male or female moose is that males have antlers and females don't. The female moose is called a cow and the male moose is called a bull. The cow and bull are similar in where they live and what they eat.

Size of a moose
When a newborn calf is born, it weighs between 25 to 30 pounds. If a calf is born in spring it can weigh 400 pounds by winter! When some moose are full grown they can weigh up to 1,800 pounds or more weighing ten times more than an average 5th grade kid! The bulls have antlers, the females don't. They can be 6 feet across and weigh up to 75–100 pounds. Moose stand at least 6 feet tall or more. They have huge bodies, but their hoof print is only 6 inches long.

Food moose eat
Moose eat a lot and the reason is, that they have four stomachs like cows and that they are so big. To find food, moose dive in a lake, as low as 18 feet for juicy pond weeds. It may sound gross to us but to them it is like Thanksgiving dinner. They also get their food from bogs, marshes, and clearings. In spring they eat twigs and leaves off trees. The mother teaches her calf what plants to eat and how to swim. Moose will eat up to 50 pounds of food in their first stomach. Then later they will regurgitate the food, re-chew it and finally swallow it again.

Enemies
Their enemies were Native American Indians. They hunted moose and used all their body parts, such as bones for tools and their fur for a blanket. People still hunt moose but today they no longer use all of their body parts because we have no need for bone tools. If moose are not attacked, they usually live as long as 15–20 years. Moose don't always die from enemies though, sometimes they die from old age or if they get a tick on them they could get very sick and die. Enemies of the moose are wolves and bears but the cow protects her calf from being attacked by lowering her head and charging. She also may kick.

Moose are amazing animals that have adapted to harsh environments and are unique animals to watch in the wild.

Bibliography
Alaska Wildlife Notebook Series. http://www.state.ak.us/adfg/notebook/biggame/moose.htm.
Book of Mammals. Volume 2, K-Z. Washington D.C.: National Geographic Society.
"Moose." World Book Encyclopedia. Volume 13. 2000.
Ritchie, Rita and Jeff Fair. The Wonder of Moose. Milwaukee, WI: Garth Stevens Publishing. 1996.

Teaching the Subgenre of the Travel Brochure

The general minilessons presented at the beginning of this chapter and the Circle of Questions strategy discussed previously will help students read and write informational texts. Using adjectives in descriptive captions and proper versus common nouns in captions are important to the specific subgenre of travel brochures.

Using Adjectives in Descriptive Captions

It is important for the author of a travel brochure to describe a place with unique adjectives. Photographs help to describe a place, as well. To demonstrate this, ask students to develop captions that use wonderful adjectives for photos provided either by you or by the students. These captions may be in the form of a sentence or a phrase. Figure 11 shows some examples of photo captions.

Using Proper Versus Common Nouns in Captions

Some nouns name specific places, persons, and things. These nouns, called *proper nouns*, are capitalized. Other nouns are common, and these are not capitalized. Present these two types of nouns together and discuss why some nouns are capitalized. The following is a list of common versus specific nouns:

oceans	Atlantic Ocean
streets	Simeon Boulevard
museums	Walker Museum
explorers	Lewis and Clark

Figure 12 shows an example of a photo caption that includes both common and specific nouns.

Reading the Travel Brochure

Before you introduce students to a travel brochure, share with them that a travel brochure is a factual account of a place containing detailed, accurate information, and is written to attract visitors to that place. A travel brochure can be designed to attract visitors to a county, state/province, or city, or to a specific attraction within a country, state/province, or city. Travel brochures about a country, state/province, or city will contain a broad descriptive statement about the place, options for places to stay (accommodations), recreational activities, and attractions.

Figure 11 Examples of Photo Captions

Slow and lumbering, a huge sea turtle comes out of the sea to lay her eggs.

Alert, watchful, and swift, the majestic pelican waits for food.

Photos ©2002 by Kathleen Buss.

Figure 12 Example of Common and Specific Nouns in a Caption

Visit Saint Vincent Island Visitor's Center, the Dixie Theatre, the Apalachicola Maritime Museum, and the John Gorrie State Museum. Don't miss the historically significant homes and the docks!

Photo ©2002 by Kathleen Buss.

Share some travel brochures with students, and as you do, ask them to make a list of adjectives and specific nouns used in the brochures. Graphic Organizer: The Travel Brochure (see Appendix A, page 100) can be used to analyze these published brochures. Figure 13 shows an example of the graphic organizer, with information from a travel brochure about Florida, USA.

Writing the Travel Brochure

The writing of a travel brochure will follow the writing process. To begin the prewriting experience, ask students to select a place that they would like to visit or a place that they have visited and know fairly well. Students then decide on a place as broad as Mexico or as specific as Acapulco. Once their place is identified, students can fill in Graphic Organizer: The Travel Brochure (see Appendix A, page 100) as their prewriting exercise. Remind students that a broad descriptive statement will introduce the reader to the place. They also can add other boxes, such as people, sports, and entertainment, to the graphic organizer. In the Children's

Figure 13 Example of the Travel Brochure Graphic Organizer

> **Place:** Fabulous Florida

> **Broad Descriptive Statement:** Fabulous Florida has it all—sultry climate, endless recreational activities, and engaging attractions.

Places to Stay:	Recreational Activities:	Attractions:
Hotels and motels	Surfing	Beaches
Resorts	Canoeing	Theme parks
Condominiums	Snorkeling	Marine labs
Lodges	Saltwater fishing	Museums
Country inns	Freshwater fishing	State parks
Bed-and-Breakfasts	Hiking	National parks
Cottages	Golfing	Gardens
	Swimming	Planetariums
Descriptions:	Shell collecting	
Luxurious		**Descriptions:**
Secluded	**Descriptions:**	Sugar-white
Spacious	Popular	Sparkling
Accommodating	Vigorous	Thrilling
Exclusive	Active	Naturalistic
Pleasant	Pleasurable	Educational
Secure	Playful	Exceptional
Liveable	Enjoyable	Scenic
	Recreational	Diverse
	Exploratory	Majestic
	Strenuous	Exciting

Literature Bibliography, there is a list of travel books that may be helpful in gathering information for students' brochures.

Once students have collected and plotted their information, they can plan how the information will be organized on a trifold brochure. The cover of their brochure should ask people to visit. Students now have five pages on which to arrange the information from their boxes. Encourage students to include photographs or pictures to illustrate their text in the brochure. The following example of a travel brochure for Mexico was written by fifth-grader Sidney:

| Mexico is a very unique country with high mountains, sandy deserts, green rainforests and sunny coasts.

Mexico is filled with sandy beaches. Parties happen all the time. | Mountains

In the mountains there are big, sharp rocks and white, cold snow. | Desert

The desert is very hot. It has sparkling sand and sharp cactus all over. |
| Rainforest

In the rainforest, you'll see wet leaves and big vines drooping, and colorful parrots. | Coast and Ocean

On the coast there are sandy beaches, bright skies, slippery seaweed, and waves moving. | Welcome to Mexico |

Summary

Studying informational books and travel brochures will expose students to how authors write to inform others about topics of interest. The Circle of Questions strategy will help build the background knowledge for reading informational text. Minilessons focusing on varying reading speeds for different purposes, understanding authors' writing and organizational style, and using photographs or illustrations to accompany the text will enhance student understanding of these texts. Asking students to write a report introduces them to using informational books to find information about a specific topic, and the same principles used by authors of informational books can be used when students write a report. The travel brochure, although not as comprehensive as the informational book, focuses on key attributes of a place of interest. Chapter 5 will cover journalistic texts and includes discussion of reading and writing news stories and advice columns.

Chapter 5

Teaching Journalistic Texts

The newspaper is a printed source in which readers find information that is current and up-to-date. Information in the newspaper is about local, state, national, or international persons and events. To help readers locate information quickly, the newspaper is divided into sections, each covering interrelated topics. The first section of the newspaper contains late-breaking news stories about the nation and the world. Also included in this section are opinion columns such as editorials and letters to the editor. Other sections include state and local news, sports, business, living and families, arts and entertainment, and classified advertisements. (For ideas for teaching the two specific subgenres of letters to the editor and classified advertisements, see chapter 6, Teaching Persuasive Texts.) Advice columns are woven throughout the sections of the paper and are correlated to the specific content of the various sections. For example, if you are seeking advice on computers, check the business section; for advice on cars, read the automotive section.

Routman (2000) states, "Being able to read, analyze, and interpret the news is part of being an informed and responsible citizen in a democracy" (p. 449). She goes on to say that as part of their education, students need to acquire the critical-thinking skills of learning about current events and how these events affect daily living. News stories provide an excellent means of reading and understanding nonfiction text. The newspaper is also an excellent starting point for learning about journalistic elements such as leads and headlines, as well as researching and reporting factual, accurate information in an unbiased manner.

In the newspaper, there are *news articles* that tell of recently occurring events and *feature articles* that are of general interest to the readership. Feature articles include sports articles; human interest articles; or reviews that provide information on movies, books, and entertainment.

The *opinion page* includes columns, such as letters to the editor and editorials, that are relevant to recent news or feature articles. These columns have a different text structure than feature articles. The question/answer format and the letter format are common structures for these columns. The sections of the paper that do not contain articles instead include comics and advertisements, such as classified and display ads, which are discussed in chapter 6.

Subgenres of journalistic texts include the following:

advice columns	international news articles
entertainment articles	local articles
business news articles	magazine articles
comics	national news articles
community news articles	sports articles
entertainment articles	stock quotes
home and garden articles	travel articles
human interest articles	weather reports

In this chapter, we will present lessons for teaching human interest articles and advice columns. We believe that students in grades 2–6 will delight in reading and writing human interest articles, and students in grades 4–6 will enjoy reading and writing advice columns.

General Journalistic Text Minilessons

The following minilessons are brief, focused lessons that teach strategies for reading and writing journalistic texts. They can be used before or during the reading of most journalistic texts.

Understanding News Article Text Structure

Because the articles in the newspaper have a different text structure than most narrative pieces that students have read, an activity that introduces the differences may be useful. In this activity, review the story structure of a narrative text with students: the title; author; introduction, which includes the setting, characters, and problem; the body of the story, which includes the actions of the characters to solve the problem; and the ending, which includes the resolution and ending. Introduce the journalistic terms and the structure of the news article to students by comparing genres of narrative text with journalistic text. Use a chart such as the one in Figure 14 to illustrate the differences and to introduce new terms.

Share with students that the *reporter* is the person responsible for gathering information and writing the journalistic article. Instead of using a title, the reporter writes a *headline* for the story. The headline is followed by the *lead*, which is an

Figure 14 Narrative Versus Journalistic Text

	Narrative—The Story	Journalistic—The Article
Writer	Author	Reporter—identified in the byline
Title	Title of story	Headline
Introduction	Setting, characters, problem	Lead—who, what, where, when, why, how
Body	Events—actions of character to solve problem	Facts—facts listed are of equal importance or the most important fact first
Ending	Resolution of problem	Summary statement—may be cut if page lacks space

introductory sentence or paragraph that answers the questions who, what, where, when, why, and how. The *body* of the article contains more details about the information given in the lead. The ending of an article is usually a *summary statement*, which may be cut if there is not enough room for it on the page.

Facts Versus Opinions

News might be defined as new, timely information about an event or person in which readers are interested. A fact is information that can be documented or verified. It is known to be true. On the other hand, opinions are personal beliefs, views, or judgments. An opinion also could be defined as what the person feels. A feeling does not make a fact no matter how many people agree with the feeling. Opinions are used in editorials and advice columns. News articles always use factual information, not opinions.

To have students better understand the difference, ask them to look through the newspaper to find examples of facts and opinions, then share them with the class. The following are examples that may be discussed:

Sports can be enjoyed as recreation. (fact)

Most people love baseball. (opinion)

The most exciting sport to watch is tennis. (opinion)

Writing Strong Leads

A lead, the first sentence or paragraph of an article, hooks the reader into reading the rest of the article. The lead also summarizes the major facts (the who, what, where, when, why, and how of the article), with the the most important fact placed first. Share the following example with students: Let's say the reporter was writing an article about the Reading Marathon at our school. The fact is that students in our school read 1,500 books. The reporter could write the lead in a number of ways. He or she could begin with a question, or begin with a quote from someone important to the article, or use a description of the setting or situation.

Have you read 1,500 books in your lifetime?

The principal says, "I am proud of all the students who read 1,500 books during the Reading Marathon."

The auditorium was quiet as Elmwood School students read for two hours on Friday.

List a group of related facts on a chart or dry-erase board at the front of the room, and invite students to experiment with building different types of leads using a question, a description, or a quote.

Expanding a Simple Sentence

Review with students that a sentence is a group of words that express a complete thought. Every sentence has two parts—a subject and a predicate:

The girls/play.

Once students are comfortable designing simple sentences, share with students that when a reporter writes an article, or especially a lead, he or she needs to provide enough detail in the sentence so that readers can picture the event or person in the article. Explain that when writing a lead, they will need to answer the questions who, what, where, when, why, and how. They can begin with a simple sentence and explore expanding these sentences until they have a lead that answers all the questions. To demonstrate, write on the chalk board the simple sentence *The girls played*, and ask the students the following questions:

1. Who were the girls?
2. What did they play?
3. Where did they play?
4. When did they play?
5. Why did they play?
6. How many girls?

Ask students to expand the sentence by inserting words that answer these questions, such as in the following example:

The three girls, who were friends, played in the baseball game for the championship title on Monday at the park.

Building Background Knowledge of Journalistic Texts

Harvey and Goudvis, in their book *Strategies That Work* (2000), suggest a strategy called Reading Like a Writer in which students are able to identify content, the reading process, and the writer's craft. This strategy could be used to study articles and columns in newspapers or magazines. Ask students to divide a piece of paper under three headings: (1) Content (facts), (2) Process (thinking), and (3) Craft (writing). In the first column, students list the facts they find when reading an article; in the second column, students list reading strategies they use, such as inference (I), questions (Q), and connections (C); in the third column, students can write down the features of an article or column. Using the article "Pen pals keep corresponding after 35 years" (Kemmeter, 1999; see Appendix B, page 105), Figure 15 shows how Reading Like a Writer might help students understand how to read and write journalistic texts.

Teaching the Subgenre of Human Interest Articles

The general minilessons presented at the beginning of this chapter and the Reading Like a Writer strategy will help students read and write human interest articles. Creating headlines and writing quotes are also helpful as specific minilessons for human interest articles.

Creating Headlines

In a few words, the headline identifies the content or significance of the article: "A headline is a summarizing phrase that captures the essence of the news story" (Buss & McClain-Ruelle, 2000, p. 28). But this phrase also must catch readers' attention, so it is written in large print and sometimes in bold letters. Students can read the article, "Pen pals keep corresponding after 35 years" (see Appendix B, page 105), then develop headlines, such as the following, that reflect the content and tone of the article:

Pen pals for life

School assignment lasts for 35 years

Two secretaries bond for 35 years

Figure 15   Example of Reading Like a Writer Strategy

Content (facts)	Process (thinking)	Craft (writing)
Pen pals have corresponded for 35 years.	*Corresponded* means writing (I). I have a pen pal. (C)	A headline is a summary, similar to a title.
The reporter is Gene Kemmeter of the *The Portage County Gazette.*		A byline tells the author's name. This one also tells the paper's name.
They began writing in 1960s.	Because they were schoolgirls, they could be around 50 now. (I)	The reporter started with the main idea.
One of the women said that their correspondence began in elementary school.	Because it was in elementary school, they are probably younger than I thought, maybe 45. (I) My elementary teacher gave us addresses for pen pals, too. (C)	This is an example of an indirect quote.

Using Quotes

Often a news article uses quotations from people interviewed. Quotes introduce the human element and help readers connect to the topic of the article. There are two types of quotations: a direct quote and an indirect quote. A direct quote surrounds the exact words of the person with quotation marks, and is attributed to the speaker, such as,

> "I am so proud of my son," said Sue Russell, mother of Billy Russell, as he hoisted the state hockey championship trophy. "Since childhood, he has always loved to skate and compete," she continued.

An indirect quote is a paraphrase of what the person said. This quote is not put in quotation marks but still needs to be credited to the speaker, such as,

> Sue Russell, mother of Billy Russell, said she was proud of her son as he hoisted the state hockey championship trophy. She said that he has always loved skating and competing.

Reading the Human Interest Article

Prior to reading the human interest article, there are certain terms and concepts that students should know. Terms that are specific to journalism relate to the people of the newsroom—*reporter, columnist, photographer, copy editor,* and *proofreader.* Share and discuss these terms with the students and, as a group, define the roles that these people play in the production of a newspaper:

- A reporter is assigned to write the news article. He or she gathers information for the article through research and interviewing.

- A columnist writes in first person and gives opinions or advice to readers.

- A photographer takes photographs that accompany articles or stand on their own as news photos.

- A copy editor checks the written article or column for mechanical or spelling errors. He or she revises and edits the article, and writes the article's headline and photo captions.

- A proofreader reads the typeset pages of the newspaper and marks additional errors to be corrected before the final paper is printed.

Tell students that a human interest article is about an experience that someone in their community has had. A newspaper reporter interviews the person to collect the facts for the article, then writes an account of the person's experience. The article is a true, accurate account of the events, and the editor of the newspaper views the article as one that will be of interest to readers.

The text structure of a human interest article is different from that of other non-fiction texts. The two organizational structures are the Inverted Pyramid and the Lead Plus Equal Facts. In an Inverted Pyramid story, after the lead, the facts of the article are ordered from most important to least important; this structure allows the editor of a newspaper to cut the end of the article if space is limited on the newspaper page. In this lesson, we will present the Lead Plus Equal Facts structure, in which the body of an article is organized around facts of equal importance, and therefore the entire article should be read (see also Buss & McClain-Ruelle, 2000).

The human interest article that will be read aloud in this lesson is "Pen pals keep corresponding after 35 years" (*The Portage County (Wisconsin) Gazette,* December 17, 1999; see Appendix B for full article). Begin by reading the headline and lead, and review the discussions from Creating Headlines and Writing Strong Leads minilessons. After the lead, the facts related to this experience are presented in the text. The body of the read-aloud article is organized in the Lead Plus Equal Facts structure, so the facts in this article follow one after the other as the story progresses.

As you read the article, ask students to complete the Graphic Organizer: The Human Interest Article (see Appendix A, page 101). Figure 16 gives an example of the graphic organizer, filled in with information from the read-aloud in this section. Ask students to browse through the local newspaper to look for other human interest articles. The students can use Graphic Organizer: The Human Interest Article to chart the organizational structure of the articles they find.

Figure 16   Example of the Human Interest Article Graphic Organizer

Headline:
Pen pals keep corresponding after 35 years.

Byline:
Gene Kemmeter
The Portage County Gazette

Lead:
In the 1960s, two school girls, one from Green Bay and the other in England, began corresponding.

Who	What	Where	When	Why	How
two school girls	write	Green Bay and England	1960– present	To communicate (inferred) Teacher gave address	Mail (inferred)

Body of Article:
Fact 1: In 1963, teacher gives Jane the address for Diane.
Fact 2: From 1963 to the present, the girls correspond.
Fact 3: Jane visits England.
Fact 4: Diane visits the United States.

Writing the Human Interest Article

Writing of the human interest article will follow the steps of the writing process. Now that students are familiar with the organizational structure of a human interest article, ask them to brainstorm a list of people in school, at home, or in the community whom they could interview to write their human interest article. For their prewriting exercise, remind students to write information from their interviews into Graphic Organizer: The Human Interest Article (see Appendix A, page 101).

The following example of a human interest article was written by a fourth-grade student, Hayliegh, for the school newspaper:

Wes's Surgery
On November 10th, Wes came back from his surgery. It was a heck of a surgery. He had to get his tonsils removed. He ate Popsicles, ice cream, and yogurt. He loved the food he got.

Wes was very nervous and very scared. He felt sore after his surgery. Wes had to chew gum after the operation because, if he didn't, his throat would be sore.

He had a lot of people visit him. The surgery took two hours. His voice was very scratchy after the surgery.

He had to stay out of school for 14 days because he probably would get an infected throat.

Wes said it was fun to stay out of school for that long. We sure missed him and we're glad to have him back!

Teaching the Subgenre of Advice Columns

The general minilessons presented at the beginning of this chapter and the Reading Like a Writer strategy will help students read and write advice columns. Narrowing the focus and creating clever signatures also are helpful as specific minilessons.

Narrowing the Focus

When an advice columnist receives a letter from a reader, the columnist narrows down the focus to the main problem. The following is an example of a letter that needs a focus:

> Dear Kid's Advisor,
>
> On my last birthday, I was 10. I had a big party with lots of my friends. We had a gorgeous pink and white cake. I got lots of presents. I loved all of them but one. I got a present that I really don't like. I know it is expensive and it's from a good friend. I don't want to hurt her feelings, but I want to return it for something I really want.
>
> Present Puzzler

Ask students to find the focus or the main problem. They will probably identify it as "I got a present that I really don't like. I know it is expensive and it's from a good friend. I don't want to hurt her feelings, but I want to return it for something I really want."

Give students examples of advice column letters such as the ones that follow, and ask them to underline the main problem or focus of each letter. Then have students locate the questions or request for advice. (All the examples of advice columns in this chapter are reprinted with permission of Highlights for Children, Inc., Columbus, Ohio, USA, Copyright ©2001.)

Dear Highlights:

When I pack my lunch for school my mom writes to me. When I take out the napkin I feel happy until my friends see it and start to laugh at me. What shall I do?

Ryshelle T., Virginia (Dear Highlights, 2001, p. 42)

Problem: embarrassed when friends see the notes my mom writes on my napkins
Question: What shall I do?

Dear Highlights:

I am better at most things than my friend. Whenever I get chosen to run in a race and he doesn't, he feels bad. What should I do?

Mosha R., Israel (Dear Highlights, 2001, p. 42)

Problem: friend feels bad when I am selected to participate in sports events and my friend is not
Question: What should I do?

Creating Clever Signatures

Instead of signing their names to a letter asking for advice, many writers compose a clever signature that identifies their problem. For instance, if a writer is having problems with friends, he or she might sign the letter "Friendless in Seattle"; if a writer feels he or she has too much homework to do every night, he or she might sign "Too Tired." After students have focused on the main questions in the examples you have given them from the newspaper, invite them to devise a clever signature for each letter.

Reading the Advice Column

Share with students that the newspaper contains columns that are written by a columnist who is an expert in a particular field. The writings of the columnist are shared with many newspapers; therefore, the newspaper buys this column to use. Advice columns are very popular. Readers of the newspapers write or e-mail a columnist for advice or recommendations on how to solve a problem. Advice columns appear in the different sections of the paper, according to the topic on which they write. For example, there are columnists such as Humberto Cruz, who writes advice on personal finance issues; James Coates, who writes advice on the use of computers; Abigail Van Buren, who writes personal advice; John Rosemond, who writes parenting advice columns; Tom and Ray Magliozzi, who write automotive advice; and Martha Stewart, who writes tips for the home and garden. Some newspapers, such as the *Tallahassee Democrat*, have teen columnists to whom students can write for advice. Some children's magazines that carry advice columns include *Highlights for Children* and *American Girl*, and *Sports Illustrated for Kids* has a regular feature called "Tips From the Pros."

Advice columns are written in a simplified letter format, with the reader's letter first followed by the columnist's answer. Share several advice columns appropriate for students in your classroom. Share with students that as they read advice columns, they should look for two things: a defined problem and a specific question or request for advice. If columnists cannot determine the question and the problem, they will have difficulty offering advice. Share the following advice column with students, and as they analyze it, ask them to fill in Graphic Organizer: The Advice Column (see Appendix A, page 102). Figure 17 shows an example of the graphic organizer filled in using text from our read-aloud advice column:

Dear Highlights
My classmate and I were best friends last year, but now he doesn't show much interest in me. Please help me out.

Curtis L., California

Sometimes people get busy with new activities and don't spend as much time with friends as they once did. That doesn't mean that they don't care anymore. When you have an opportunity, talk to your friend alone. Tell him that you miss spending time with him. Then listen to what he has to say. It is possible that he is upset with you, but he may just be going through a busy time. By talking about the situation, the two of you may find ways to spend more time together. (Dear Highlights, 2001, p. 42)

Writing the Advice Column

The writing of an advice column will follow the writing process. Students can fill in Graphic Organizer: The Advice Column (see Appendix A, page 102) as a prewriting exercise.

Ask for student volunteers to be the columnists and student volunteers to be readers asking for advice. Types of personal questions that could be written are personal advice on friends, family, allowance, cooking, baby-sitting, school, homework, computers, and hobbies. Review with students that when writing a letter to an advice columnist, they must give background of a particular event or situation that troubles them and pose their problem in a form of a question or request for advice.

Figure 17   Example of the Advice Column Graphic Organizer

> Dear Highlights (name of columnist):

> **Problem (posed by reader):**
> My classmate and I were best friends last year, but now he doesn't show much interest in me.
>
> **Question or Request for Advice:**
> Please help me out.
>
> **Signed (name of reader asking advice):**
> Curtis L., California
>
> **Summary of Problem:**
> classmate doesn't seem to be best friend anymore

> **Dear Curtis L.:**
> **Answer (from columnist):**
> Sometimes people get busy with new activities and don't spend as much time with friends as they once did. That doesn't mean that they don't care anymore.
> When you have an opportunity, talk to your friend alone. Tell him that you miss spending time with him. Then listen to what he has to say. It is possible that he is upset with you, but he may just be going through a busy time. By talking about the situation, the two of you may find ways to spend more time together.

The following example was written by a sixth grader who has had a lot of experience traveling the globe. She has spoken to groups of children who are about to move to another country with their parents, and the following is a question she often receives:

Dear World Traveler,
My family and I are moving overseas. I am excited but I'm kind of nervous and scared. I don't want to leave my friends. Can you tell me how I can make new friends?

Friendless Mover

Dear Friendless Mover,
You will miss your friends but you can stay in touch with them. Most expatriots in other countries have gone through this so it will be pretty easy to make friends. They will know how you feel and be excited to become your friend.

Morgan

Summary

The newspaper is full of text written for different purposes and using various text structures. In this chapter, we have touched on very different purposes and structures found within the newspaper—Lead Plus Equal Facts and the simplified letter format—by introducing human interest articles and advice columns. Using these two text types, we have taught about a news article researched and written by a reporter. The advice column merges the reader of the newspaper and a columnist. The minilessons that we presented concentrated on developing an awareness of journalistic text, the content of news articles, and writing styles of reporters and columnists. We hope that students will use this knowledge as they read other parts of the newspaper seeking current information about their city, state, country, and world. Our next chapter focuses on teaching persuasive text, the most powerful genre of nonfiction.

Chapter 6

Teaching Persuasive Texts

There are many types of persuasive texts that can reach a variety of audiences. The main purpose of persuasive texts is to present an argument or an opinion in an attempt to convince the reader to accept the writer's point of view. Reading and reacting to the opinions of others helps shape readers' beliefs about important issues, events, people, places, and things.

Persuasive texts also are written to persuade the reader to do something, buy something, or believe something. The subgenres presented in this section represent a sampling of the varieties of persuasive texts that elementary students can explore by both reading and writing. We invite you to add to this list to meet the needs of your instructional program.

Persuasive pieces that can be found in the newspaper include classified advertisements, display advertisements, editorials, and letters to the editor. *Classified advertisements* are listed in a special section of the newspaper with an appropriate heading and are often referred to as Want Ads. These are ads sent to the newspaper by its readers. The headings of these ads include Help Wanted, Rentals, For Sale, Pets, Houses for Sale or Rent, and Lost and Found. *Display advertisements* appear throughout the newspaper. These ads can be printed on a portion of a page or on an entire page, and they usually contain pictures and prices of items. Stores or corporations purchase this ad space to sell their products.

Editorials are written by the editor of the newspaper, who selects an issue of interest to the readers and presents arguments for or against this issue. The editor may use opinions, facts, and rhetorical questions to convince readers of his or her point of view. The readers of the newspaper write *letters to the editor* in which they state an opinion, ask a question about a previous newspaper article or editorial, or respond to a previous letter to the editor. Letters to the editor usually are related to the newspaper's content.

Other types of persuasive texts can be found in informational books, political speeches, persuasive letters and memos, and persuasive essays. A person who argues either for or against an issue, attempting to persuade readers to vote a certain way in an election or to accept the writer's point of view, writes these pieces. Authors of *persuasive informational books* use accurate facts about their topic to sway readers to believe their point of view. *Political speeches, persuasive letters* and *memos,* and *persuasive essays* are written to persuade others to accept the author's point of view and take action for a particular person or cause.

Subgenres of persuasive texts include the following:

apologies	letters to the editor
billboards	letters of protest
book reviews	letters of complaint
campaign speeches	memos
classified advertisements	movie reviews
critiques	music reviews
debates	persuasive essays
display advertisements	persuasive informational books
editorials	posters
essays	real estate descriptions
job applications	sales pitches

This chapter will present in-depth lessons for reading and writing classified advertisements and persuasive books, letters, and political speeches. We feel that an effective way to introduce students in grades 2–4 to persuasive text is through classified advertisements. Students in grades 4–6 can study more complicated types of persuasive texts such as persuasive letters and political speeches.

General Persuasive Texts Minilessons

The following minilessons are brief, focused lessons that teach strategies for reading and writing persuasive texts. They can be used before or during the reading of most persuasive texts.

Using Techniques of Persuasion

Discuss the concept of persuasion with students. Ask them to identify ways to persuade that are most effective in written persuasions. One persuasive technique is to appeal to logic, in which authors try to make readers identify and analyze the point of view taken and its rationale. This technique might include posing a problem and then suggesting a solution using accurate, logically organized facts. Subgenres that use appeal to logic include editorials, campaign speeches, and debates.

The second persuasive technique is to appeal to admiration and transfer. With this technique, readers can identify with a spokesperson or group, such as a celebrity or attractive, successful people. Authors who use this technique hope that readers also will see themselves as well-known, attractive, wealthy, or successful if they buy services or products or accept the ideas presented. Subgenres that use appeal to admiration and transfer include display advertisements and classified advertisements.

A third persuasive technique is to appeal to the emotions, often called the bandwagon approach, in which the author presents information in such a way to make readers believe that many others feel the same way. It is difficult for readers not to get swept up by this type of persuasive technique, especially when a sense of urgency to take action is presented. The use of animals, rewards, and rhetorical questions is common with this technique. Subgenres that use an appeal to emotion technique include display advertisements, campaign speeches, and letters of protest.

A fourth persuasive technique is to appeal to readers' senses. Writers hope that slogans and catchy sayings, music and sound effects, and the repetition of claims and product names catch readers' attention. Subgenres that use appeal to the senses include billboards, posters, advertisements, and movie and music reviews.

Using Strong Helping Verbs

Share with students that authors sometimes use strong helping or auxiliary verbs to add voice or mood to the main verb. Such helping verbs include *will, should, must, have, do, are, can, did,* or *be.* Present to students the following quotes from famous speeches, drawing notice to the use of strong helping verbs used by the writers to stress their messages.

From Abraham Lincoln's Emancipation Proclamation, September 22, 1862:

> And by virtue of the power and for the purpose aforesaid, I do order and declare that all persons held as slaves within said designated States and parts of States are, and henceforth shall be, free; and that the Executive Government of the United States, including the military and the naval authorities thereof, will recognize and maintain the freedom of said persons. (Lincoln, as cited in Miller, 1999, p. 72)

From George W. Bush's Speech to Joint Session of Congress and U.S. Citizens, September 20, 2001:

> The advance of human freedom—the great achievement of our time and the great hope of every time—will lift a dark threat of violence from our people and our future. We will rally the world to this cause by our efforts and by our courage. (Bush, as cited in "Bush lives up," 2001, p. B3)

Building a Strong Message Using Repetitive Phrases

Share with students that often when a speaker or writer wants to build emotion and create a dramatic mood, he or she repeats phrases to persuade others to action. Share some of the following repetitive phrases with students.

From the Declaration of Sentiments, written by men and women attending the Seneca Falls Convention, July 20, 1848:

> The history of mankind is a history of repeated injuries and usurpations on the part of man toward woman, having in direct object the establishment of an absolute tyranny over her. To prove this, let facts be submitted to a candid world.
> He has never permitted her to exercise her inalienable right to the elective franchise. He has compelled her to submit to laws, in the formation of which she had no voice. He has withheld from her rights which are given to the most ignorant and degraded men—both natives and foreigners. (cited in Miller, 1999, pp. 61–62)

From Franklin Delano Roosevelt's War Message to Congress, December 8, 1941:

> Yesterday the Japanese government also launched an attack against Malaya. Last night Japanese forces attacked Hong Kong. Last night Japanese forces attacked Guam. Last night Japanese forces attacked the Philippine Islands. Last night the Japanese attacked Wake Island. (Roosevelt, as cited in Miller, 1999, pp. 107–108)

From John F. Kennedy's Inaugural Address, January 20, 1961:

> Let both sides explore what problems unite us instead of belaboring those problems which divide us. Let both sides, for the first time, formulate serious and precise proposals for the inspection and control of arms—and bring the absolute power to destroy other nations under the absolute control of all nations. Let both sides seek to invoke the wonders of science instead of its terrors. Together let us explore the stars, conquer the deserts, eradicate disease, tap the ocean depths, and encourage the arts and commerce. (Kennedy, as cited in Miller, 1999, p. 117)

From Martin Luther King, Jr.'s March on Washington "I Have a Dream" Address, August 28, 1963:

> I say to you today, my friends, that in spite of the difficulties and frustrations of the moment I still have a dream. It is a dream deeply rooted in the American dream.

I have a dream that one day this nation will rise up and live out the true meaning of its creed: "We hold these truths to be self-evident; that all men are created equal."

I have a dream that one day on the red hills of Georgia the sons of former slaves and the sons of former slaveowners will be able to sit down together at the table of brotherhood.

I have a dream that one day even the state of Mississippi, a desert state sweltering with the heat of injustice and oppression, will be transformed into an oasis of freedom and justice.

I have a dream that my four little children will one day live in a nation where they will not be judged by the color of their skin but by the content of their character.

I have a dream today. (King, as cited in Miller, 1999, p. 135)

Students also may notice repetitive words in advertisements. Places such as countries, states, and resorts, as well as product names and telephone numbers, are often repeated so we will remember them.

Building Background Knowledge for Persuasive Texts

RAFT stands for role, audience, format, and topic (Santa & Havens, 1995). Modified for teaching persuasive texts, RAFT is a particularly good choice for building background knowledge. This strategy encourages students to read and write persuasive texts effectively by asking the following questions:

Who is the writer?

Who is the intended audience?

What is the form of the writing?

What is the topic of the piece, and what techniques are used to persuade or convince?

Using an excerpt from a persuasive letter written by Abigail Adams, RAFT might be used as follows:

I long to hear that you have declared an independency—and by the way in the new Codes of Laws which I suppose it will be necessary for you to make I desire you would Remember the Ladies, and be more generous and favorable to them than your ancestors. Do not put such unlimited power into the hands of the Husbands. Remember all Men would be tyrants if they could. If particular care and attention is not paid to the Ladies we are determined to foment a Rebellion, and will not hold ourselves bound by any Laws in which we have no voice, or Representation. (Adams, as cited in Miller, 1999, p. 17)

Who is the writer? Abigail Adams

Who is the intended audience? John Adams, her husband, who was a participant at the drafting committee for the Declaration of Independence. He was later to become our second president.

What is the form of writing? A persuasive personal letter

What is the topic, and what are the persuasive techniques used? Abigail Adams wanted women to be represented in the Declaration of Independence. She wanted women to be given the opportunity to vote. The techniques she uses are strong helping verbs such as *would* and *will,* comparatives of *more generous* and *favorable,* generalized participants such as *the Ladies, the Husbands, all Men,* and she also uses a not-so-subtle threat of fomenting a *Rebellion.* (See minilesson "Using Different Types of Adjectives" that follows for more about comparatives.)

When students write a persuasive text, they can use the same questions. Post the following questions, as well as brief explanations of them, in the classroom for reference:

Who is the writer? Will you write as a concerned student, or a citizen of the United States or of the world, or as an environmentalist?

Who is your audience? Audience is crucial. When writing a persuasive piece, you must keep your audience in mind at all times. Questions to ask yourself include, How do I want my audience to respond to this text? Is my audience a potential buyer or a concerned citizen?

What is the form of writing? The persuasive genre is varied. You must choose the most effective form to get your message across to your audience.

What is the topic of your piece, and what persuasive techniques will help convey your opinions to your intended audience? You must be clear about your topic. Not having a clear persuasive stance will weaken your argument. Your choice of the intended audience may help you determine the persuasive techniques that will be most effective.

Teaching the Subgenre of Classified Advertisements

The general previous minilessons and the RAFT strategy will help students read and write classified advertisements. Using the comparative and superlative forms of adjectives and using rhetorical questions are also helpful, specific minilessons for teaching classified advertisements.

Using Different Types of Adjectives

Share with students that when reading or writing a persuasive piece, authors use different types of adjectives. There are adjectives that are positive (such as *pretty, good, frisky,* and *friendly*); there are comparatives that compare two things (such as *prettier, better, friskier,* and *friendlier*); and there are superlatives that show the highest degree or that compare three or more things (such as *prettiest, best, friskiest,* and *friendliest*). Share with students that when authors attempt to persuade others, they will often use adjectives that show that their product, item, or idea is the best. Students, as they read persuasive pieces, can start a word wall for the different types of adjectives using the categories Positive, Comparative, or Superlative.

Explain to students that adding *er* forms some comparatives and adding the word *more* forms others (such as *crunchier* and *more flavorful*). Adding *est* forms some superlatives, and adding the word *most* forms others (such as *crunchiest* and *most flavorful*). Writers do not use the words *more* or *most* with a word that already ends in the comparative or superlative form.

Words that are most difficult for students are those that are exceptions to the above rules. Presenting these adjectives in their positive forms and then having students find their comparative and superlative forms might be helpful (*good–better–best* and *bad–worse–worst* and *many–more–most*). A good place to search for these adjectives is in advertisements. People would not be interested in an ad for a good product, item, or idea. They want only the best, or at least the better of two products, items, or ideas.

Using Rhetorical Questions

Students may think of questions as types of sentences that need answers. Explain to students that some writers use rhetorical questions that the reader is not expected to stop and answer, nor will the writer necessarily pause to answer. A writer may use rhetorical questions to get the reader to think about a personal connection to the topic and to begin to formulate questions or thoughts related to the topic. Although rhetorical questions are used in most persuasive pieces of writing, a good place to locate them is in advertisements. Questions such as "Do you want brighter teeth in three weeks?" or "Do you need more money?" imply a need for a product or service.

Reading the Classified Advertisement

Give students the opportunity to examine classified advertisements in the local newspaper. Invite students to make a list of all the different categories of classified ads they find, which might include Pets and Supplies, Arts and Crafts, Antiques and Collectibles, Musical Instruments, Toys and Games, Sporting Goods, Real Estate, Lost/Found, Tickets and Travel, and Services Offered. Remind students that classified ads are placed and paid for by the readers of the newspaper either to sell something, to find something that was lost, or to buy something.

Ask students to share some of these ads with a partner and look for the following information: what is being advertised, description of product or service, price, and contact person. Ask students to list descriptive adjectives that the writers use in the ad to convince readers that they are purchasing a quality product or service.

Have students categorize types of persuasion used, such as appeal to logic, appeal to admiration and transfer, appeal to emotions, and appeal to the senses (see the first general minilesson in this chapter). The following examples of classified advertisements were written to sell something, to ask for help in finding something lost, or to offer services. Share them with students, and ask students to fill in Graphic Organizer: The Classified Advertisement (see Appendix A, page 103) to chart the advertisement and identify the type of persuasion used by the author. (Note: Not all the ads shared in this section include prices.) Figure 18 gives an example of the graphic organizer, filled in using information from our read-aloud of the classified ads:

For Sale—Pets & Supplies

Cocker spaniel: AKC, quality, rare colors, Excellent temperament, great with kids. $300, 715-xxx-xxxx.

Chocolate lab pups for sale. Family raised, exceptional breeding, champion bloodlines, happy, friendly, parents excellent hunters. $350 each, 608-xxx-xxxx.

Figure 18   Example of the Classified Advertisement Graphic Organizer

Item being sold: cocker spaniel **Description:** Appeal to Admiration: AKC [American Kennel Club] Appeal to Emotions: great with kids, excellent temperament Appeal to Logic: quality Appeal to Senses: rare colors **Price:** $300 **Contact Person:** phone number	**Item being sold:** chocolate lab pups **Description:** Appeal to Admiration: champion bloodline Appeal to Emotions: friendly, happy Appeal to Logic: breeding, excellent hunting parents **Price:** $350 each **Contact Person:** phone number

The following are some examples of classified advertisements from the book *The Roman News: The Greatest Newspaper in Civilization* (Langley & De Souza, 1997).

IDEAL HOME!

Beautify your home with colorful mosaic flooring. We use the best quality stone or glass pieces, laid into a sturdy plaster base. Patterns or pictures—hunting scenes a specialty.

The Decorators, beside the Theatre of Pompey, Rome (p. 26)

WIGS GALORE

Wigs and hairpieces for every occasion. Made from the finest blond hair cut from barbarian slave girls.

The Head Works, by Trajan's Forum, Rome (p. 18)

The following is an example of a lost-and-found advertisement written by Abraham Lincoln:

March 26, 1836

FROM a stable in Springfield, on Wednesday, 18th a large bay horse, star in his forehead, plainly marked with harness; supposed to be eight years old; had been shod all round, but is believed to have lost some of his shoes, and trots and paces. Any person who will take up said horse, and leave information at the Journal office, or with the subscriber at New-salem, shall be liberally paid for their trouble. A. LINCOLN. (Lincoln, 1953; reprinted with permission by the Abraham Lincoln Association)

And Then What Happened, Paul Revere? (Fritz, 1998) shares an advertisement written by Paul Revere when he was attempting to find ways to make money by becoming a dentist. The ad reads, "Artificial Teeth. Paul Revere, He fixes them in such a Manner that they are not only an Ornament, but of real Use in Speaking and Eating" (p. 14).

Invite students to find and read other types of classified advertisements, and ask students to chart the information found in these advertisements using the graphic organizer presented in Appendix A, page 103. Tell students they also can add to their word wall of positive, comparative, or superlative adjectives.

Writing the Classified Advertisement

Writing classified advertisements will follow the process of writing. Students can fill in Graphic Organizer: The Classified Advertisement (see Appendix A, page 103) as a prewriting exercise. Students first will need to determine a list of items they would like to advertise. Looking at the four techniques of persuasion, ask students to determine which they will use. They may use all four techniques if they wish. Have the students make a list of descriptive adjectives that they will use in their ad. Encourage students to use some of the information from the general and specific minilessons you have modeled. Invite students to write text for display advertisements, as well.

The following classified advertisement was written by Cory, grade 4:

For Sale: German Shepherd Pups
Vet says healthy and strong, jet black with tan, always alert, playful, and loving to kids. AKC Champion breed. 3 males and 4 females, call soon; these will sell fast. $250. Call Cory 555-xxx-xxxx.

The following display advertisement was written by second grader Megan:

CARB BONE FOR DOGS
This is a bone that is very helpful to your dog's teeth. It is also a bone that comes in different flavors. You are most likely to find it at a pet store or at a store like Wal-Mart.

So if your dog's breath is smelling badly, go get a carb bone. Your dog will love the taste and will love to chew it up. Chances are, you will be getting another bone.

Teaching the Subgenres of Persuasive Informational Books, Letters, and Political Speeches

The general minilessons and the RAFT strategy will help students read and write persuasive texts such as persuasive informational books, letters, and political speeches. Also helpful are the specific minilessons for these subgenres: using generalized audiences and "specific you" and using little words.

Using Generalized Audience and "Specific You"

Writers of persuasive texts want to influence as many people as possible, so they write to a very broad, generalized audience. For example, a U.S. politician might begin a speech with the phrase *Fellow Americans*. Some other words and phrases that suggest a generalized audience include *everyone* and *concerned citizens*.

But writers of persuasive texts also use the very specific word *you*. The generalized audience has caught the reader's attention as part of this large group of people, and now the writer wants to persuade the most important person directly—you. Erlbach, in her book *The Kid's Volunteering Book* (1998), uses both the generalized audience and the "specific you" techniques:

> Have you ever wanted to make a difference? Have you ever wanted to help someone, or be a part of an effort to change the world? If so, you are like plenty of other kids. Millions of young people, just like you, have volunteered their time and talents. They have helped people, animals, and the environment. (p. 6)

The following is an example of both the generalized audience and the specific you techniques, from John F. Kennedy's Inaugural Address, January 20, 1961: "And so, my fellow Americans: ask not what your country can do for you—ask what you can do for your country" (Kennedy, as cited in Miller, 1999, p. 118).

Using Little Words That Say What You Mean

Persuasive texts do not need to be long-winded to be effective. In the book *Great Grammar Lessons That Work: Using Poems, Picturebooks, Games, and Writing Activities to Teach Grammar and Help Students Become Better Writers*, Karnowski (2000) writes that as students use longer words in their speech and learn to use the thesaurus, they may write more sophisticated words when meaning might dictate the use of small ones. A minilesson focusing on the use of small words by famous U.S. presidents will make this technique clear to students.

Explain that when speechwriters use small words and short sentences, their message is made stronger because the text is simple and precise, therefore easily understood by more people. To demonstrate this point, tell students that John F. Kennedy's Inaugural Address of 1961 was brief—only 1,350 words long. Besides being brief, however, Kennedy's speechwriter took a cue from another president, Abraham Lincoln, and used short words. Miller (1999) puts it this way:

> Kennedy asked his speechwriter to discover the "secret" of Lincoln's Gettysburg Address, which he hoped to use as a model. The speechwriter reported to him, "Lincoln never used a two- or three-syllable word where a one-syllable word would do, and never used two or three words where one word would do." (p. 115)

Thus, Kennedy's much-quoted sentence—"And so, my fellow Americans: ask not what your country can do for you—ask what you can do for your country"—had tremendous impact.

Reading Persuasive Informational Books, Letters, and Political Speeches

Share with students that authors of persuasive pieces start with an introduction that presents their position, argument, or opinion on a topic. Next, authors present at least three pieces of evidence that support their opinion or position. Authors may choose to present their strongest argument first, or they may decide to put the strongest argument last. Finally, authors conclude the piece by restating or summarizing their position or calling for the reader to act.

Read aloud the persuasive informational book *Be a Friend to Trees* (Lauber, 1994), in which the author gives reasons why trees are important and why we should protect them. As you read this book to students, have them map out the elements of a persuasive piece by filling in Graphic Organizer: The Persuasive Informational Book, Letter, or Political Speech (see Appendix A, page 104). Figure 19 provides an example of the graphic organizer that has been filled in using the book *Be a Friend to Trees*.

Figure 19   Example of the Persuasive Informational Book Graphic Organizer

---

Position/Argument: Be a Friend to Trees

Supporting Evidence:
1. Everything that is made of wood was once part of a tree. (p. 8)
2. Paper also comes from trees. (p. 10)
3. Some trees can be tapped for their sap. (p. 11)
4. You eat the parts of trees known as fruits and nuts... (p. 13)
5. Many animals eat parts of trees known as fruits and nuts. (p. 14)
6. Many animals make their homes in trees. (p. 18)
7. The roots of trees hold soil in place. (p. 21)

Concluding Statement:
Much of the oxygen that people and animals need comes from trees. Without them, we might not be here at all. So trees are more than nice—they're something we can't live without!
And that is why everyone should be a friend to trees. (p. 29)

The following read-aloud is an example of a persuasive letter, written by President Theodore Roosevelt in 1908 to the State Department after a visit from the ambassador from China. Share the example with students, and have them map out the text structure of the letter using the Graphic Organizer: The Persuasive Informational Book, Letter, or Political Speech (see Appendix A, page 104). Figure 20 shows the graphic organizer filled in for this read-aloud.

Washington, December 2, 1908

To the Department of State: I wish to find out from the Department why it permitted the Chinese Ambassador today twice to use the phrase "Your Excellency" in addressing the President. Not only law but wise custom and propriety demand that the President shall be addressed only as "Mr. President" or as "the President." It is wholly improper to permit the use of a silly title like "Excellency" (and incidentally if titles were to be allowed at all, this title is entirely unworthy of the position of the President). Any title is silly when given the President. This title is rather unusually silly. But it is not only silly but inexcusable for the State Department, which ought, above all other Departments, to be correct in its usage, to permit foreign representatives to fall into the blunder of using this title. I would like an immediate explanation of why the blunder was permitted and a statement in detail as to what has been done by the Department to prevent the commission of any similar blunder in the future. (Roosevelt, 1908)

Figure 20   Example of the Persuasive Letter Graphic Organizer

Position/Argument:
To find out from the Department why it permitted the Chinese ambassador today twice to use the phrase "Your Excellency" in addressing the President

Supporting Evidence:
1. Not only law but wise custom and propriety demand that the President shall be addressed only as "Mr. President" or as "the President."
2. It is wholly improper to permit the use of a silly title like "Excellency."
3. But it is not only silly but inexcusable for the State Department, which ought, above all other Departments, to be correct in its usage, to permit foreign representatives to fall into the blunder of using this title.

Concluding Statement:
I would like an immediate explanation of why the blunder was permitted and a statement in detail as to what has been done by the Department to prevent the commission of any similar blunder in the future.

Writing Persuasive Informational Books, Letters, and Political Speeches

Now students should be ready to begin to write the draft of their persuasive pieces following the process of writing. Students can use Graphic Organizer: The Persuasive Informational Book, Letter, or Political Speech (see Appendix A, page 104) as a prewriting exercise. Explain that the written piece can be a letter, a memo, or a speech. First, students will need to decide on their topic, their position on this topic, and their audience, then have them fill in the graphic organizer to plan their first draft.

The following student example of a persuasive letter was written by Sara, a fifth grader:

Dear Governor,

I believe that the Minnesota state star should be the North Star.

First, I believe that the North Star would be a good state symbol because we are called the North Star State and our tip is the farthest north of 49 states.

Another reason why I think the North Star would be a good state symbol is that everybody in the state can see it outdoors. You don't have to pay to see it like the Timberwolves or Vikings so it would be cheaper.

Finally, I believe the North Star would be a good state symbol because it would be very good for people to learn about stars. When more people know about stars that helps our country's space station NASA.

Governor, I believe that the North Star should be the star of Minnesota because we are called the North Star State, everyone can see it outdoors, and we need to learn about stars.

Sincerely, Sara

Summary

This chapter has presented persuasive texts that elementary students will enjoy exploring as they learn how authors attempt to sway readers to a particular point of view. Students were introduced to persuasive techniques and language patterns authors use as they craft their position on a topic. By being introduced to the persuasive subgenre of classified advertisements, younger students observe how authors manipulate words and language to build a strong message and encourage their readers to relate to their thoughts. Older students were encouraged to analyze persuasive texts as they explore how authors craft powerful language to persuade or present arguments through persuasive informational books, letters, or political speeches.

This chapter concludes our discussion of reading and writing nonfiction. We have included texts throughout this book that we felt students in grades two through six would enjoy exploring as they seek and share information. The texts presented represent only a sampling of available nonfiction texts. It is our hope that if students have authentic experiences with nonfiction texts, their interest in further study of the purposes and text structures of nonfiction will be aroused.

Graphic Organizers

Graphic Organizer: The Biography

Introduction:
Birth   Setting   Family

Events:

1.

2.

3.

4.

5.

6.

7.

8.

9.

10.

Conclusion:

Reading and Writing Nonfiction Genres by Kathleen Buss and Lee Karnowski © 2002. Newark, DE:
International Reading Association. May be copied for classroom use only.

Introductory Statement:

Who   What   Where   When   Why

Sequence of Events:

1.

2.

3.

4.

5.

6.

7.

8.

Closing Statement (optional):

Title:

Yield:

Time:

Ingredients:

Equipment (optional):

Procedure:

Title of Game:

Number of Players:

Equipment (what we need):

Goal:

How to Play (rules of the game):

Variations (optional):

Title:

Introduction to Topic (optional):

A—word, phrase, or sentence with A:

Descriptive sentence or paragraph:

B—word, phrase, or sentence for B:

Descriptive sentence or paragraph:

Conclusion (optional):

Title:

Introduction:

The Cycle

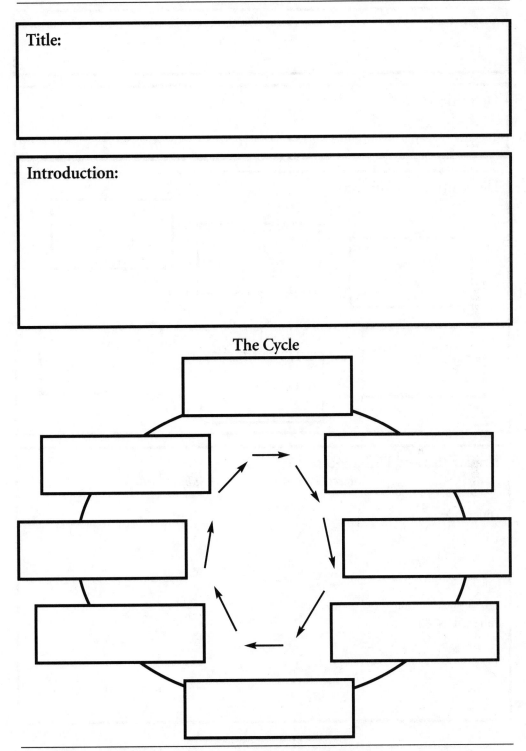

Graphic Organizer: The Report

Title:

Definition:

Descriptions of Subject:

Topic:

Similarities and Differences:

Subject   Subject

Differences

Similarities

(continued)

Problems and Solutions:

Problems	Solutions
1.	1.
2.	2.
3.	3.

Cause and Effect:

Cause	Effect
1.	1.
2.	2.
3.	3.

Sequence of Events or Information:

1.

2.

3.

4.

5.

6.

Place:

Broad Descriptive Statement:

Places to Stay:	Recreational Activities:	Attractions:
Descriptions:	Descriptions:	Descriptions:

Headline:

Byline:

Lead:
Who   *What*   *Where*   *When*   *Why*   *How*

Body of Article:

Fact 1.

Fact 2.

Fact 3.

Fact 4.

Fact 5.

Fact 6.

Graphic Organizer: The Advice Column

Dear (name of columnist):_____

Problem (posed by reader):

Question or Request for Advice:

_____

_____

_____

_____

Signed (name of reader asking advice): _____

Summary of Problem:_____

_____

_____

_____

_____

Dear _____:

Answer (from columnist):

_____

_____

_____

_____

_____

_____

_____

_____

_____

Item to sell, service offered, or item to buy:

Description (descriptive words used to persuade):

Appeal to Logic:

Appeal to Admiration and Transfer:

Appeal to Emotions:

Appeal to Senses:

Price:

Contact Person:

Graphic Organizer: The Persuasive Informational Book, Letter, or Political Speech

Position/Argument:

Supporting Evidence:

1.

2.

3.

4.

Concluding Statement:

Human Interest Article

Pen pals keep corresponding after 35 years

by Gene Kemmeter

The Portage County Gazette (Wisconsin, USA), December 17, 1999. Reprinted with permission.

In the 1960's, two schoolgirls, one in Green Bay and the other in England, began corresponding.

More than 35 years later, the two continue to write, although the time between their writing each other has shrunk, courtesy of e-mail.

Jane Goudreau, 157 W. Clark St., was that student in Green Bay, while Diane Goodson, Dover, England, was her British counterpart.

Goudreau said the correspondence began after her elementary school teacher gave her Diane's address in 1963.

They wrote about daily life, Goudreau said, and kept in touch. Their correspondence through the years reflected changes in technology, going from writing, to sending audio tapes and now to e-mail via computers and the Internet.

In 1981, Jane and her husband, Jack, went for a visit, then Jane went back alone in 1985.

That 1985 visit was also the subject of one of the first "Country Samplers" written by the late John Anderson in the Stevens Point Journal.

Around the Fourth of July, Diane made her first trip to the United States, bringing her son, Jonathan, 21, with her. They stayed in Stevens Point and made some trips around the state, including to Green Bay to meet with Goudreau's family.

Through the years, they corresponded about changes in their lives, marriages, buying homes, jobs and births of sons. Jane has a son, Brion, 23, while Diane has a son, Jonathan.

Both are secretaries. Jane works for the Stevens Point Area Public School District while Diane works for a chemical company.

Goudreau said the vibrancy in their communications has kept them together through the years, along with the idiosyncrasies of the language of their countries.

Part of that, she said, is reflected in a recent e-mail from Diane. Goudreau said she closed out an e-mail by saying she had to get something done "before the snow flies." Diane wrote back asking what snow flies are.

Goudreau said she wrote back, trying to explain the phrase, but wonders if Diane understands.

Below are some questions posed to Goodson about her visit to Stevens Point and Wisconsin during the Fourth of July. Her responses are in their entirety, giving the reader a flavor of the correspondence that Goudreau has treasured for so many years, as well as British spellings for some words.

Was this your first trip to the United States?
Yes! A trip that had been looked forward to, for so many years!

What differences did you observe between your country and here?
1. The vastness of the land! The extremely long and straight roads that seemed to go on forever! The roads are very wide too. (English roads are very narrow in comparison!)
2. U.S.A. houses—the majority seem to be made of wood. It's very rare to find a wooden house in England. It was interesting to see hardly any house was of the same design! Very varied in construction. In England, you have streets full of the same "type/style" of house—to the point of being boring!
3. In the U.S., electrical goods are cheaper! Food is about a third cheaper. Petrol (gas) is especially cheap!!!! Clothes were very reasonable too, especially Levi jeans (jeans in general)! The English always stock up on the jeans when visiting the U.S.! In general, the cost of living in the U.S. is much lower than in G.B. (Great Britain).
   *Point of interest—Wal-Mart bought out one of our major supermarkets ("ASDA") this summer and since this has happened, all the other major supermarkets have begun to drop their prices quite dramatically. About time too!! We have been ripped off for far too long. Being an island, we have to take what comes, it seems until the good U.S. of A. comes to our rescue!!
4. We observed that people don't seem to walk to their destinations!! In England, you can walk down town to do shopping! In Stevens Point, we took the car—but as Jane said, the shops are not situated closely together, as they are in a typical English town. We think people walk more in England though!
5. We noticed that every town has a water tower with the name of the town painted on it.
6. Steak …!! Jonathan and I actually ate American beef!! In England, we had "mad cow disease" (this passes onto humans—called "CJD"). The media did

a good job on the coverage of this awful outbreak, consequently, Jonathan and I never eat beef in England! (The majority of people now eat beef, since the situation has been given the "all clear"). Jack was determined to make us eat American beef and cooked a "mean" fillet steak for me and a rare T-bone for Jonathan. It was so, so delicious, that I asked Jack to cook another one before we returned back to England, as I knew, it would be the last time we ate beef—until returning to the U.S., that is!!!

Is life more hectic here than in Britain, or did it just seem that way because of the short time you were here?
We never noticed life being hectic, far from it—that may be because we visited at a public holiday time—July the 4th celebrations! It was really nice to help you celebrate too! In general, the pace of life seemed about the same as England. We come from a provincial part of England, no doubt the cities are a "rat race" in both countries.

Was there one thing that you remember most about your visit here?
Yes. The friendliness shown and the hospitality of the people. I personally found it very touching and will never forget it. American people are more "open" than us reserved English.

You started your pen-pal relationship in the 1960's as school children. What do you attribute the long-lasting nature of this continuing relationship to?
Probably due to the fact that Jane and I have a lot in common and can "talk the hind leg off a donkey" about all and everything—albeit now by e-mail!!
1. We are of similar age (I'm the older one—but don't tell everyone!)
2. Our sense of humor interacts very well!
3. We each had a son and have followed closely, their progress.
4. Earlier, when we were writing as kids, there was always the mystery and excitement that "one day we would meet." Jane was the first to be able to visit me in England. Since the visits (Jane has visited me twice) it has made the bond even stronger.
5. We have now met out respective families (aunties, uncles, cousins, and friends—the whole shabang!!!) And we both know that we "belong" as one of the family. After all these years of contact, it's almost like "returning home."

What do you write about most often?
Just life in general. What each other have done the past week, or have planned in the future etc.

Now that computers have become more common, how often do you correspond via e-mail?

We correspond on a regular basis, more so when there is a lot of news to impart. The cost of e-mail in England is higher than the U.S., so we have to budget ourselves, otherwise, the phone bill would be horrendous!! British telecom are contemplating their prices and hopefully, they may be going down soon—so, look out Jane!!

Do you find that speed better to keep informed?

Yes, absolutely. We have corresponded even more regularly since e-mail and have kept up to date with news, instead of getting news that is "old hat!" It's possible to write more by e-mail, as it allows you to write about incidences that occurred in recent times, rather than having to think about the past (for letter writing) much more easily.

References

Bomer, R. (1995). *Time for meaning: Crafting literate lives in the middle and high school.* Portsmouth, NH: Heinemann.

Buss, K., & Karnowski, L. (2000). *Reading and writing literary genres.* Newark, DE: International Reading Association.

Buss, K., & McClain-Ruelle, L. (Eds.). (2000). *Creating a classroom newspaper.* Newark, DE: International Reading Association.

Calkins, L.M. (1994). *The art of teaching writing* (New ed.). Portsmouth, NH: Heinemann.

Elbow, P. (1973). *Writing without teachers.* New York: Oxford University Press.

Fritz, J. (1996, Spring/Summer). *Research tells the story.* CBC Features, 49(1), n.p.

Graves, D. (1994). *A fresh look at writing.* Portsmouth, NH: Heinemann.

Harvey, S., & Goudvis, A. (2000). *Strategies that work: Teaching comprehension to enhance understanding.* York, ME: Stenhouse.

Heller, M.F. (1995). *Reading-writing connections: From theory to practice* (2nd ed.). White Plains, NY: Longman.

Karnowski, L. (2000). *Great grammar lessons that work: Using poems, picturebooks, games, and writing activities to teach grammar and help students become better writers.* New York: Scholastic.

Langer, J.A. (1981). From theory to practice: A prereading plan. *Journal of Reading, 25,* 152–156.

Langer, J.A. (1982). Facilitating text processing: The elaboration of prior knowledge. In J.A. Langer & M.T. Smith-Burke (Eds.), *Reader meets author/bridging the gap: A psycholinguistic and sociolinguistic perspective* (pp. 149–162). Newark, DE: International Reading Association.

Lewis, M., & Wray, D. (1995). *Developing children's non-fiction writing: Working with writing frames.* Leamington Spa, UK: Scholastic.

Lewis, M., Wray, D., & Rospigliosi, P. (1995). "No copying, please!" Helping children respond to non-fiction text. *Education 3–13, 23,* 27–34.

Miller, M. (1999). *Words that built a nation.* New York: Scholastic.

Moss, B. (1995). Using children's nonfiction trade books as read-alouds. *Language Arts, 72,* 122–126.

Pappas, C., Kiefer, B., & Levstik, L. (1990). *An integrated perspective in the elementary school: Theory into action.* New York: Longman.

Routman, R. (2000). *Conversations: Strategies for teaching, learning, and evaluating.* Portsmouth, NH: Heinemann.

Sampson, M.B., Sampson, M.R., & Linek, W. (1994–1995) Circle of questions. *The Reading Teacher, 48,* 364–365.

Santa, C.M., Havens, L.T., & Maycumber, E.M. (1995). *Creating independence through student-owned strategies.* Dubuque, IA: Kendall/Hunt.

Sloan, P., & Latham, R. (1988). *Text types and the teaching of reading and writing.* Paper presented at the Genre Workshop, Perth, Western Australia.

Tompkins, G.E. (2000). *Teaching writing: Balancing process and product* (3rd ed.). Upper Saddle River, NJ: Merrill.

Vaughan, J.L., & Estes, T.H. (1986). *Reading and reasoning beyond the primary grades.* Boston: Allyn & Bacon.

Wing, J.L. (1991). *Write ways: Modeling writing forms.* New York: Oxford University Press.

Zinsser, W. (Ed.). (1987). *Inventing the truth: The art and craft of memoir.* Boston: Houghton Mifflin.

Children's Literature Bibliography

Chapter 1: Teaching Recounts

Biographies

Anderson, W. (1998). *Pioneer girl: The story of Laura Ingalls Wilder.* New York: HarperCollins.

Bierman, C., & Hehner, B. (1998). *Journey to Ellis Island: How my father came to America.* Ill. L. McGaw. New York: Hyperion.

Blumberg, R. (1993). *Bloomers!* Ill. M. Morgan. New York: Macmillan.

Brighton, C. (1999). *The fossil girl: Mary Anning's dinosaur discovery.* Brookfield, CT: Millbrook.

Carlson, L. (1998). *Boss of the plains: The hat that won the West.* Ill. H. Meade. New York: DK Ink.

Collins, D.R. (1990). *Pioneer plowmaker: A story about John Deer.* Ill. S. Michaels. Minneapolis: Carolrhoda.

Conrad, P. (1991). *Prairie visions: The life and times of Solomon Butcher.* New York: HarperCollins.

Cooney, B. (1996). *Eleanor.* New York: Viking.

Crouch, T.D. (1989). *The bishop's boys: A life of Wilbur and Orville Wright.* New York: Norton.

Fradin, D. (1997). *Mary Anning: The fossil hunter.* Ill. T. Newsom. Parsippany, NJ: Silver Press.

Freedman, R. (1987). *Lincoln: A photobiography.* New York: Clarion.

Freedman, R. (1991). *The Wright Brothers: How they invented the airplane.* New York: Holiday House.

Freedman, R. (1992). *An Indian winter.* Ill. K. Bodmer. New York: Holiday.

Freedman, R. (1997). *Out of darkness: The story of Louis Braille.* Ill. K. Kiesler. New York: Scholastic.

Freedman, R. (1998). *Martha Graham: A dancer's life.* New York: Clarion.

Fritz, J. (1969). *George Washington's breakfast.* Ill. P. Galdone. New York: Coward-McCann.

Fritz, J. (1973). *And then what happened, Paul Revere?* New York: Coward-McCann.

Fritz, J. (1974). *Why don't you get a horse, Sam Adams?* New York: Putnam.

Fritz, J. (1999). *Why not, Lafayette?* Ill. R. Himler. New York: Putnam.

Hoyt-Goldsmith, D. (1998). *Lacrosse: The national game of the Iroquois.* Ill. L. Migdale. New York: Holiday .

Krull, K. (1996). *Wilma unlimited: How Wilma Rudolph became the world's fastest woman.* Ill. D. Diaz. San Diego: Harcourt Brace.

Medearis, A.S. (1997). *Princess of the press: The story of Ida B. Wells-Barnett.* New York: Lodestar.

Pinkney, A. (1996). *Bill Pickett: Rodeo-ridin' cowboy.* Ill. B. Pinkney. New York: Voyager.

Sandberg, C. (1985). *Abe Lincoln grows up.* San Diego: Harcourt Brace.

Sis, P. (1996). *Starry messenger: Galileo Galilei.* New York: Farrar, Straus & Giroux.

Memoirs

Chall, M.W. (1992). *Up north at the cabin.* Ill. S. Johnson. New York: Lothrop, Lee & Shepard.

Cooney, B. (1990). *Hattie and the wild waves: A story from Brooklyn.* New York: Viking.

Coy, J. (1996). *Night driving.* Ill. P. McCarty. New York: Henry Holt.

Cross, V. (1992). *Great-grandma tells of threshing day.* Morton Grove, IL: Albert Whitman.

de Paola, T. (1989). *Art lesson.* New York: Putnam.

de Paola, T. (1999). *26 Fairmount Avenue.* New York: Putnam.

de Paola, T. (2000). *Here we all are.* New York: Putnam.

de Paola, T. (2001). *On my way.* New York: Putnam.

de Paola, T. (2002). *What a year.* New York: Putnam.

Dorros, A. (1991). *Abuela.* Ill. E. Kleven. New York: Dutton.

Hendershot, J. (1987). *In coal country.* Ill. T. Allen. New York: Knopf.

Herrera, J.F. (1995). *Calling the doves: El canto de las palomas.* Ill. E. Simmons. San Francisco: Children's Book Press.

Igus, T. (1996). *Two Mrs. Gibsons.* Ill. D. Wells. San Francisco: Children's Book Press.

Ippisch, H. (1998). *Sky: A true story of courage during World War II.* Mahwah, NJ: Troll.

Levinson, R. (1990). *I go with my family to grandma's.* Ill. D. Goode. New York: Dutton.

Peterson, C. (1999). *Century farm: One hundred years on a family farm.* Ill. A. Upitis. Honesdale, PA: Boyds Mills Press.

Pinkney, G.J. (1992). *Back home.* Ill. J. Pinkney. New York: Dial.

Rylant, C. (1982). *When I was young in the mountains.* Ill. D. Goode. New York: Dutton.

Rylant, C. (1985). *The relatives came.* Ill. S. Gammell. New York: Bradbury.

Rylant, C. (1989). *But I'll be back again: An album.* New York: Orchard.

Rylant, C. (1991). *Appalachia: The voices of sleeping birds.* Ill. B. Moser. San Diego: Harcourt Brace Jovanovich.

Thomas, J.R. (1988). *Saying goodbye to grandma.* New York: Clarion.

Yolen, J. (1987). *Owl moon.* Ill. J. Schoenherr. New York: Philomel.

Autobiographies

Aliki. (1998). *Marianthe's story: Painted words: Spoken memories.* New York: Greenwillow.

Bitton-Jackson, L. (1997). *I have lived a thousand years: Growing up in the holocaust.* New York: Simon & Schuster.

Bridges, R. (1999). *Through my eyes.* New York: Scholastic.

Bruchac, J. (1997). *Bowman's store: A journey to myself.* New York: Dial.

Cole, J., & Saul, W. (1996). *On the bus with Joanna Cole: A creative autobiography.* Portsmouth, NH: Heinemann.

George, J.C. (1996). *The tarantula in my purse and 172 other wild pets.* New York: HarperCollins.

Lobel, A. (1998). *No pretty pictures: A child of war.* New York: Greenwillow.

Parks, R., & Haskins, J. (1997). *I am Rosa Parks.* Ill. W. Clay. New York: Dial.

Polacco, P. (1998). *Thank you, Mr. Falker.* New York: Philomel.

Personal Journals, Diary Entries, Personal Letters, and Postcards

Armstrong, J. (2001). *Dear Mr. President: Theodore Roosevelt letters from a young coal miner.* New York: Winslow.

Bently, J. (1997). *"Dear friend": Thomas Garrett & William Still, collaborators on the underground railroad.* New York: Cobblehill.

Dragisic, P. (1998). *How to write a letter.* New York: Franklin Watts.

Filapovia, Z. (1994). *Zlata's diary: A child's life in Sarajevo.* New York: Penguin.

Frank, A. (1952). *The diary of a young girl.* New York: Simon & Schuster.

George, J.C. (1998). *Look to the North: A wolf pup diary.* Ill. L. Washburn. New York: HarperCollins.

Johnson, D. (1994). *Seminole diary: Remembrances of a slave.* New York: Macmillan.

Olson, S., & Jacobsson, A. (2001). *In Ned's head.* New York: Atheneum.

Parks, R. (1996). *Dear Mrs. Parks: A dialogue with today's youth.* New York: Lee and Low.

Rappaport, D. (1999). *The flight of Red Bird: The life of Zitkala-Sa.* New York: Puffin.

Ryan, C. (Ed.). (1993). *Louisa May Alcott: Her girlhood diary.* Ill. M. Graham. New York: Troll.

Talbot, H., & Greenberg, M. (1996). *Amazon diary: The jungle adventures of Alex Winters*. New York: Putnam.

Turner, A. (1997). *Mississippi mud: Three prairie journals*. Ill. R. Blake. New York: HarperCollins.

Van der Rol, R., & Verhoeven, R. (1995). *Ann Frank: Beyond the diary: A photographic remembrance*. New York: Scott Foresman.

Webb, S. (2000). *My season with the penguins: An Antarctic journal*. Boston: Houghton Mifflin.

Wilder, L.I., & Lane, R.W. (1994). *On the way home: The diary of a trip from South Dakota to Mansfield, Missouri, in 1894*. New York: HarperTrophy.

Chapter 2: Teaching Procedural Texts

Recipe Books

Baird, P. (1999). *Cooking with Mickey and friends*. New York: Disney.

Bass, J. (1999). *Cooking with Herb, the vegetarian dragon: A cookbook for kids*. Ill. D. Harte. New York: Barefoot Books.

Cobb, V. (1994). *Science experiments you can eat*. Ill. D. Cain. New York: HarperCollins.

D'Amico, J., & Drummond, K.E. (1994). *The science chef: 100 fun foods experiments and recipes for kids*. New York: Wiley.

D'Amico, J., & Drummond, K.E. (2000). *The United States cookbook: Fabulous foods and fascinating facts from all 50 states*. New York: Wiley.

Jones, J., & Jones, E. (1998). *Knead it, punch it, bake it!: The ultimate breadmaking book for parents and kids*. New York: Houghton Mifflin.

Katzen, M. (1999). *Honest pretzels and 64 other amazing recipes for cooks ages 8 & up*. Berkeley, CA: Tricycle.

Walker, B. (1979). *The Little House cookbook: Frontier foods from Laura Ingalls Wilder's classic stories*. Ill. G. Williams. New York: HarperCollins.

Game Rules

Clark, B. (1997). *Kids' book of soccer: Skills, strategies, and the rules of the game*. Ill. T. Stokes. Secaucus, NJ: Carol Publishing Group.

Cole, J., & Calmenson, S. (1998). *Marbles: 101 ways to play*. Ill. A. Tiegreen. New York: William Morrow.

Erlbach, A. (1997). *Sidewalk games around the world*. Ill. S. Holm. Brookfield, CT: Millbrook.

Fox, P. (1997). *Classic outdoor games: All the rules, all the classics*. Palo Alto, CA: Klutz.

Gryski, C. (1998). *Let's play: Traditional games of childhood*. Ill. D. Petricic. Buffalo, NY: Kids Can Press.

Healy, D. (1995). *The illustrated rules of baseball*. Ill. P. McRae. Nashville, TN: Ideals Children's Books.

Jaffe, E., Field, S., & Labbo, L. (2002). *Games around the world: Dominoes*. Minneapolis: Compass Point Books.

Jaffe, E., Field, S., & Labbo, L. (2002). *Games around the world: Hopscotch*. Minneapolis: Compass Point Books.

Jaffe, E., Field, S., & Labbo, L. (2002). *Games around the world: Jacks*. Minneapolis: Compass Point Books.

Jaffe, E., Field, S., & Labbo, L. (2002). *Games around the world: Marbles*. Minneapolis: Compass Point Books.

Johnson, A.A. (1995). *String games from around the world*. Palo Alto, CA: Klutz.

Perez, E. (2000). *100 Best games*. Ill. M. Rius. Hauppauge, NY: Barron's.

How-To Books

Aliki. (1986). *How a book is made.* New York: HarperCollins.

Ancona, G. (1994). *The piñata maker/El Piñatero.* San Diego: Harcourt Brace.

Carlson, L. (1993). *EcoArt: Earth-friendly art and craft experiences for 3- to 9-year-olds: A Williamson Kids Can! book.* Charlotte, Vermont: Williamson Publishers.

Carter, D.A. (1999). *The elements of pop-ups: A book for aspiring paper engineers.* New York: Simon & Schuster.

Charles, O. (1988). *How is a crayon made?* Englewood Cliffs, NJ: Prentice Hall.

Hendry, L., & Rebnord, L. (1999). *Making picture frames.* Toronto: Kids Can Press.

Hoyt-Goldsmith, D. (1990). *Totem pole.* Ill. L. Migdale. New York: Holiday House.

Jones, G. (1995). *My first book of how things are made: Crayons, jeans, peanut butter, guitars, and more.* New York: Scholastic.

Klutz & The Metropolitan Museum of Art. (Eds.). (2000). *A book of artrageous projects.* Palo Alto, CA: Klutz.

Kneissler, I. (2000). *Super simple origami.* New York: Sterling.

Kohl, M.A., & Gainer, C. (1991). *Good earth art: Environmental art for kids.* Bellington, WA: Bright Ring.

Lewis, B.A. (1998). *The kid's guide to social action.* Minneapolis: Free Spirit.

Morris, A. (1994). *How teddy bears are made: A visit to the Vermont Teddy Bear factory.* Ill. K. Heyman. New York: Scholastic.

Smolinski, J. (2000). *The first-timer's guide to origami.* Los Angeles: Lowell House Juvenile.

Steltzer, U. (1995). *Building an igloo.* New York: Holt.

Chapter 3: Teaching Sequentially Ordered Texts

ABC Books

Bennett, A., & Kessler, J. (1996). *Apples, bubbles, and crystals: Your science ABC's.* Ill. M. Sarecky. New York: McGraw Hill.

Brown, P. (1995). *African animals ABC.* San Francisco: Sierra Club.

Butler, D.H. (1998). *M is for Minnesota.* Ill. J. Porter. Minneapolis: University of Minnesota Press.

Cheney, L. (2002). *A patriotic primer.* Ill. R. Glasser. New York: Simon & Schuster.

Chial, D., Anderson, H., & Bach, J.S. (1994). *M is for Minnesota (my states alphabet book).* Minneapolis: Voyageur Press.

Chin-Lee, C. (1997). *A is for Asia.* Ill. Y. Heo. New York: Orchard Books.

Johnson, S.T. (1996). *Alphabet city.* New York: Viking.

Jordon, M., & Jordan, T. (1996). *Amazon alphabet.* New York: Kingfisher.

Kalman, B. (1997). *Community helpers from A to Z.* New York: Crabtree.

Kalman, B. (1997). *Musical instruments from A to Z.* New York: Crabtree.

Kalman, B. (1999). *ABSea.* Topeka, KS: Econo-Clad.

Knowlton, J. (1998). *Geography from A to Z: A picture glossary.* Ill. H. Barton. New York: HarperCollins.

Mayers, F.C. (1994). *Baseball ABC.* New York: Harry N. Abrams.

McCurdy, M. (1998). *The sailor's alphabet.* Boston: Houghton Mifflin.

Mullins, P. (1993). *V for vanishing: An alphabet of endangered animals.* New York: HarperCollins.

Pallotta, J. (1986). *The icky bug alphabet book.* Ill. R. Masiello. Watertown, MA: Charlesbridge.

Pallotta, J. (1986). *The ocean alphabet book.* Ill. F. Mazzola. Watertown, MA: Charlesbridge Publishing.

Pallotta, J. (1991). *The underwater alphabet book.* Ill. E. Stewart. Watertown, MA: Charlesbridge.

Pallotta, J. (1996). *The fresh water alphabet book.* Ill. D. Biedrzycki. Watertown, MA: Charlesbridge.

Pallotta, J., & Stillwell, F. (1997). *The airplane alphabet book.* Ill. R. Bolster. Watertown, MA: Charlesbridge.

Pratt, K.J. (1992). *A walk in the rainforest.* Nevada City, CA: Dawn.

Pratt, K.J. (1994). *A swim through the sea.* Nevada City, CA: Dawn.

Tapahonso, L. (1995). *Navajo ABC: A dine alphabet book.* New York: Macmillan.

Wargin, K. (2000). *L is for Lincoln: An Illinois alphabet.* Ill. G. van Frankenhuyzen. Chelsea, MI: Sleeping Bear Press.

Cycle Books

Guiberson, B.Z. (1991). *Cactus hotel.* Ill. M. Lloyd. New York: Henry Holt.

Heilgman, D. (1996). *From caterpillar to butterfly.* Ill. B. Weissman. New York: Harper Trophy.

Himmelman, J. (2000). *A hummingbird's life.* Chicago: Children's Press.

Hooper, M. (1998). *The drop in my drink: The story of water on our planet.* Ill. C. Coady. New York: Viking.

Kalman, B., & Smithyman, K. (2002). *The life cycle of a bird.* New York: Crabtree.

Lasky, K. (1993). *Monarchs.* Ill. C. Knight. San Diego: Harcourt Brace.

Legg, G. (1998). *From caterpillar to butterfly.* Ill. C. Scrace. London: Franklin Watts.

Morris, J. (1993). *Animal-go-round.* New York: Dorling Kindersley.

Peterson. C. (1996). *Harvest year.* Ill. A. Upitis. Honesdale, PA: Boyds Mills.

Pfeffer, W. (1997). *A log's life.* Ill. R. Brickman. New York: Simon & Schuster.

Pringle, L. (1997). *An extraordinary life: The story of a monarch butterfly.* Ill. B. Marstall. New York: Orchard.

Scrace, C. (1999). *The journey of a butterfly.* New York: Franklin Watts.

Trumbauer, L. (2002). *The life cycle of a salmon.* Mankato, MN: Pebble Books.

Chapter 4: Teaching Informational Texts

Informational Books

Arnold, C. (1996). *Bat.* New York: Morrow.

Arnold, C. (1997). *Hawk highway in the sky: Watching raptor migration.* Ill. R. Kruidenier. San Diego: Harcourt Brace.

Arnosky, J. (1986). *Deer at the brook.* New York: Lothrop, Lee & Shepard.

Arnosky, J. (1987). *Racoons and ripe corn.* New York: Lothrop, Lee & Shepard.

Arnosky, J. (1995). *All about owls.* New York: Scholastic.

Arnosky, J. (1995). *Otters under water.* New York: Putnam.

Arnosky, J. (1996). *All about deer.* New York: Scholastic.

Arnosky, J. (2001). *All about turtles.* New York: Scholastic.

Beeler, S.B. (1998). *Throw your tooth on the roof: Tooth traditions from around the world.* Ill. G. Karas. Boston: Houghton Mifflin.

Berman, R. (1992). *American bison.* Ill. C. Bellville. Minneapolis: Carolrhoda.

Bowen, B. (1998). *Tracks in the wild.* Boston: Houghton Mifflin.

Branley, F.M. (2000). *The international space station.* Ill. T. Kelley. New York: HarperCollins.

Cherry, L. (1996). *A river ran wild: An environmental history.* Boston: Houghton Mifflin.

Cowley, J. (1999). *Red-eyed tree frog.* Ill. N. Bishop. New York: Scholastic.

Darling, K. (1996). *Rain forest babies.* New York: Walker.

Esbensen, B.J. (1994). *Baby whales drink milk.* Ill. L. Davis. New York: HarperCollins.

Evert, L. (2000). *Wolves*. Ill. J. McGee. Minnetonka, MN: NorthWord.

Geisert, B., & Geisert, A. (1999). *River town*. Boston: Houghton Mifflin.

Gibbons, G. (1995). *Sea turtles*. New York: Holiday House.

Gibbons, G. (1997). *The honey makers*. New York: HarperCollins.

Gibbons, G. (1998). *Penguins!* New York: Holiday House.

Gibbons, G. (1998). *Soaring with the wind: The bald eagle*. New York: Morrow.

Gibbons, G. (2000). *Apples*. New York: Holiday House.

Goldin, A. (1999). *Ducks don't get wet*. Ill. H. Davie. New York: HarperCollins.

Griffey, H. (1998). *Volcanoes and other natural disasters*. New York: Dorling Kindersley.

Hoban, T. (1997). *Construction zone*. New York: Greenwillow.

Hodge, D. (1998). *Simple machines*. Ill. R. Boudreau. Buffalo, NY: Kids Can Press.

Hunter, R.A. (1998). *Cross a bridge*. Ill. E. Miller. New York: Holiday House.

James, E., & Barkin, C. (1998). *How to write super school reports*. New York: Beech Tree.

Kalbacken, J. (1996). *Badgers*. New York: Children's Press.

Kalman, B., & Everts, T. (1994). *Frogs & toads*. New York: Crabtree.

Kalman, B., & Langille, J. (2000). *What is an amphibian?* New York: Crabtree.

Kuhn, B. (1999). *Angels of mercy: The army nurses of World War II*. New York: Atheneum.

Lasky, K. (2001). *Interrupted journey: Saving endangered sea turtles*. Ill. C. Knight. Cambridge, MA: Candlewick.

Latimer, J.P., & Nolting, K.S. (1999). *Backyard birds*. Ill. R. Peterson. Boston: Houghton Mifflin.

Lauber, P. (1986). *Volcano: The eruption and healing of Mount St. Helens*. New York: Simon & Schuster.

Lauber, P. (1990). *An octopus is amazing*. Ill. H. Keller. New York: Cronwell.

Lauber, P. (1996). *Hurricanes: Earths mightiest storms*. New York: Scholastic.

Lauber, P. (1999). *What you never knew about fingers, forks, and chopsticks*. Ill. J. Manders. New York: Simon & Schuster.

Ling, M., & Atkinson, M. (2000). *The snake book*. New York: Dorling Kindersley.

Lourie, P. (2000). *Mississippi River: A journey down the father of waters*. Honesdale, PA: Boyds Mills.

Maass, R. (1997). *Tugboats*. New York: Holt.

Maestro, B. (1993). *The story of money*. Ill. G. Maestro. New York: Clarion.

Maestro, B., & Maestro, G. (1994). *Bats: Night fliers*. New York: Scholastic.

Martin, J. (1993). *Tentacles: The amazing world of octopus, squid, and their relatives*. New York: Crown.

Micucci, C. (1997). *The life and times of the peanut*. Boston: Houghton Mifflin.

Miller, D. S. (2000). *River of life*. Ill. J. Van Zyle. New York: Clarion.

Murphy, J. (2000). *Blizzard! The storm that changed America*. New York: Scholastic.

Parker, N.W. (1996). *Locks, crocs, & skeeters: The story of the Panama Canal*. New York: Greenwillow.

Patent, D.H. (1998). *Homesteading: Settling America's heartland*. Ill. W. Munoz. New York: Walker.

Penny, M. (2000). *Polar bear: Habitats, life cycles, food chains, threats*. Austin, TX: Raintree Steck-Vaughn.

Petersen, D. (2001). *The Gulf of Mexico*. New York: Children's Press.

Pringle, L. (1995). *Coral reefs: Earth's undersea treasures*. New York: Simon & Schuster.

Rauzon, M.J., & Bix, C.O. (1994). *Water, water everywhere*. San Francisco: Sierra Club.

Ripley, C. (1995). *Why is soap so slippery? And other bathtime questions*. Ill. S. Ritchie. Toronto: Owl.

Rounds, G. (1999). *Beaver*. New York: Holiday House.

Shaw, N. (1999). *Bats*. Mankato, MN: Creative Education.

Simon, S. (1999). *Crocodiles and alligators*. New York: HarperCollins.

Simon, S. (1999). *The brain: Our nervous system.* New York: Mulberry.

Stewart, M. (2001). *Fishes.* New York: Children's Press.

Thimmesh, C. (2000). *Girls think of everything: Stories of ingenious inventions by women.* Ill. M. Sweet. Boston: Houghton Mifflin.

Winner, C. (2001). *Bison.* Ill. J. McGee. Minnetonka, MN: NorthWord.

Wright-Frierson, V. (1999). *A North American rain forest scrapbook.* New York: Walker.

Travel Books

Armbruster, A. (1996). *A true book of Lake Superior.* New York: Children's Press.

Countries of the World series, Bridgestone Books, available at http://www.capstone-press.com

January, B. (1999). *A true book: Ireland.* New York: Children's Press.

Keller, K.T. (2002). *Camping: The great outdoors.* Mankato, MN: Press.

Krull, K. (1997). *Wish you were here: Emily's guide to the 50 States.* Ill. A. Schwartz. New York: Doubleday.

Landau, E. (1999). *A true book: Australia and New Zealand.* New York: Children's Press.

Leigh, N. (1993). *Learning to swim in Swaziland: A child's eye-view of a southern African country.* New York: Scholastic.

Minor, W. (1998). *Grand Canyon: Exploring a natural wonder.* New York: Blue Sky Press.

Munro, R. (2001). *The inside-outside book of New York City.* New York: SeaStar Books.

Munro, R. (2001). *The inside-outside book of Washington, D.C.* New York: SeaStar Books.

Peterson, D. (2001). *A true book: National Parks.* New York: Children's Press.

Pluckrose, H. (1998). *France.* London: Franklin Watts.

Pluckrose, H. (2001). *Germany.* London: Franklin Watts.

Wright-Frierson, V. (1996). *A desert scrapbook: Dawn to dusk in the Sonoran Desert.* New York: Simon & Schuster.

Zubot, C., & Blackstock, L. (1999). *Discovering today's Japan (the discovery series).* New York: Oxford University Press.

Question-and-Answer Books

Berger, M., & Berger, G. (1999). *How do flies walk upside down? Questions and answers about insects.* Ill. J. Effler. New York: Scholastic.

Berger, M., & Berger, G. (2000). *Do all spiders spin webs? Questions and answers about spiders.* Ill. R. Osti. New York: Scholastic.

Berger, M., & Berger, G. (2001). *How do bats see in the dark? Questions and answers about night creatures.* Ill. J. Effler. New York: Scholastic.

Berger, M., & Berger, G. (2001). *What do sharks eat for dinner? Questions and answers about sharks.* Ill. J. Rice. New York: Scholastic.

Chinery, M. (1999). *Questions and answers about polar animals.* Ills. J. Butler & B. McIntyre. New York: Kingfisher.

Cummings, P., & Cummings, L. (1998). *Talking with adventurers: Conversations with Christina Allen, Robert Ballard, Michael Blakey, Ann Bowles, Jane Goodall, Dereck and Beverly Joubert.* Washington, DC: National Geographic Society.

O'Neill, A. (1996). *I wonder why snakes shed their skin and other questions about reptiles.* London: Kingfisher.

Theodorou, R. (1994). *I wonder why triceratops had horns and other questions about dinosaurs.* New York: Kingfisher.

Wangberg, J.K. (1997). *Do bees sneeze? And other questions kids ask about insects.* Ill. E. Parker. Golden, CO: Fulcrum.

White, N. (1997). *Why do cats do that?* Ill. G. Fiammenghi. New York: Scholastic.

Guidebooks

Burns, D.L. (1995). *Trees, leaves, and bark.* Minocqua, WI: NorthWord.

Cassie, B. (2000). *National Audubon Society first field guide: Shells.* New York: Scholastic.

Dudley, K. (1998). *Bald eagles.* Austin, TX: Raintree Steck-Vaughn.

Forshaw, J., Howell, S., Lindsey, T., & Stallcup, R. (1995). *The Nature Company guides: Birding.* San Fancisco: Time Life Books.

Hamilton, K. (1997). *The butterfly book: A kid's guide to attracting, raising, and keeping butterflies.* Santa Fe, NM: John Muir.

Ladd, D. (1995). *Tallgrass prairie wildflowers.* Ill. F. Oberle. Helena, MT: Falcon Press.

Lambert, M. (1997). *DK Pockets: Reptiles.* New York: Dorling Kindersley.

Latimer, J., & Notling, K.S. (2000). *Peterson Field Guides for young naturalists: Butterflies.* Ill. A. Wright. Boston: Houghton Mifflin.

Smith, C.L. (2000). *National Audubon Society first field guide: Fishes.* New York: Scholastic.

Tekiela, S. (1998). *Birds of Minnesota field guide.* Cambridge, MN: Adventure Publications.

Wilson, C. (1998). *National Audubon Society first field guide: Insects.* New York: Scholastic.

Chapter 5: Teaching Journalistic Texts

Books and Articles

Bentley, N., & Guthrie, D. (1998). *The young journalist's book: How to write and produce your own newspaper.* Ill. K. Arnsteen. Brookfield, CT: Millbrook.

Crosby, D. (1994). *Create your own class newspaper.* Nashville, TN: Incentive Publications.

Dear Highlights. (2001, October). *Highlights for children,* p. 42.

Englart, M.R. (2001). *Newspapers: From start to finish.* Ill. J. Sobiech. Woodbridge, CT: Blackbirch.

Kemmeter, G. (1999, December 17). Pen pals keep corresponding after 35 years. *The Portage County (Wisconsin) Gazette,* 1, 13.

Langley, A., & DeSouza, P. (1996). *The Roman news: The greatest newspaper in civilization.* New York: Scholastic.

Leedy, L. (1990). *The furry news: How to make a newspaper.* New York: Holiday House.

News Sources and Magazines for Children

American Girl Magazine, PO Box 37311, Boone, IA 50037-2311. http://www.americangirl.com

Cobblestone Publications, 30 Grove Street, Suite C, Peterborough, NH 03458, USA. http://www.cobblestonepub.com (Nonfiction magazines include *Appleseeds* [grades 2–4], *Ask* [grades 2–4], *Click* [grades 1–2], *Spider* [grades 1–4], *Calliope* [grades 4 and up], *Cobblestone* [grades 4 and up], *Dig* [grades 4 and up], *Faces* [grades 4 and up], *Footsteps* [grades 4 and up], *Muse* [grades 4 and up], and *Odyssey* [grades 4 and up].)

Highlights for Children, 803 Church Street, Honesdale, PA 18431. http://www.highlights.com

Kids Discover, 149 Fifth Avenue, New York, NY 10010.

National Geographic World, published by National Geographic Society, 1145 17th Street NW, Washington, DC 20036. http://www.nationalgeographic.com/world

Ranger Rick, published by the National Wildlife Federation, 11100 Wildlife Center Drive, Reston, VA 20190-5362. http://www.nwf.org/kids/

Sports Illustrated for Kids, published by Time, Inc., 135 West 50th Street, New York, NY 10020-1393. http://www.sikids.com

Time for Kids, published by Time, Inc., 1271 6th Avenue, 25th Floor, New York, NY 10020. http://www.timeforkids.com

Zillions: Consumer Reports for Kids, published by Consumer Union of U.S., Inc., 101 Truman Avenue, Yonkers, NY, 10703-1057. http://www.zillions.org/

Zoobooks Magazine, published by Wildlife Education Ltd., 12233 Thatcher Court, Poway, CA, 92064-6880. http://zoobooks.com

Chapter 6: Teaching Persuasive Texts

Persuasive Informational Books

Bang, M. (2000). *Nobody particular: One woman's fight to save the bays.* New York: Henry Holt.

Berger, M. (1994). *Oil spill!* Ill. P. Mirocha. New York: HarperCollins.

Erlbach, A. (1998). *The kids' volunteering book.* Minneapolis, MN: Lerner.

Hill, L.S. (1997). *Parks are to share.* Minneapolis, MN: Carolrhoda.

Lauber, P. (1994). *Be a friend to trees.* Ill. H. Keller. New York: HarperCollins.

Other Persuasive Writing

Burleigh, R. (1997). *Who said that? Famous Americans speak.* Ill. D. Catrow. New York: Henry Holt.

Bush lives up to his pledge to be "uniter." (2001, September 20). *Wisconsin State Journal* [Editorial]. p. B3.

Holzer, H. (2000). *Abraham Lincoln: The writer. A treasury of his greatest speeches and letters.* Honesdale, PA: Boyds Mills.

King, M.L. (1997). *I have a dream.* New York: Scholastic.

Lincoln, A. (1953). Advertisement for a lost horse. In R.P. Basler (Ed.), *Collected works of Abraham Lincoln* (Vol 1., http://www.hti.umich.edu/l/lincoln/). Springfield, IL: Abraham Lincoln Association.

Miller, M. (1999). *Words that built a nation: A young person's collection of historic American documents.* New York: Scholastic.

Philip, N. (1997). *In a sacred manner I live: Native American wisdom.* Boston: Houghton Mifflin.

Roosevelt, T. (1908). To the State Department. In *United States Postal Service unforgettable letters.* Retrieved June 6, 2002 from http://www.usps.com/letters/volume2/pres08.html

The URLs for websites change as the sites are updated and reconfigured. Usually, if the URL has changed, an alternative address will be posted. If the URL has changed, typing the name of the website in an Internet search will direct you to the correct website.

Children's Literature Websites

Carol Hurst's Children's Literature Site
http://www.carolhurst.com/authors/authors.html
> This website contains links to authors' websites and information for author studies in the classroom.

The Children's Literature Web Guide
http://www.acs.ucalgary.cal/~dkbrown
> This useful Web guide includes links to author websites as well as ideas for teaching author studies.

KidSpace@The Internet Public Library
http://www.ipl.org/kidspace
> This website contains useful information for children, teachers, and parents, and includes pages called Reference, The World, Reading Zone, and Fun Stuff.

Vandergrift's Children's Literature Page
http://scils.rutgers.edu/%7Ekvander/ChildrenLit/index.html
> At this website, you will find over 300 links to author and illustrator websites. It also includes multiple bibliographies of books such as children's cookbooks, informational resources, and multicultural children's stories.

Content Area Reading and Writing Websites

Audubon Online—National Audubon Society
http://www.audubon.org
> This site is designed specifically for kids, with pages such as "Watch List," "List of State Birds." There is also a "Teacher's Corner."

Automated Weather Service
http://www.aws.com/aws_2001/schools

This site contains geographically specific weather just a zip code away. Current local and national weather is available. Students can use the interactive weather lessons that use mapping and graphing tools.

Bridge—Ocean Sciences Teacher Resource Center
http://www.vims.edu/bridge

An extensive website devoted to the marine sciences, this site features scores of links to other websites that deal with oceanography and other ocean science topics. Teachers will find many lesson plans and thematic units for all grades.

Education World: History Center
http://www.educationworld.com/history

This site, which contains lesson plans, themes, and standards, allows teachers to focus on a specific period in history (such as Prehistoric, Ancient History, Early World, Modern World, or the United States) they wish to teach.

Enature.com
http://www.enature.com

Organized like a guidebook, this website contains a massive amount of information about U.S. wildlife such as native plants, seashells, and amphibians. Site viewers may also go on an extended search, or e-mail questions to the experts associated with this site.

The History Place
http://www.historyplace.com

This is a well-organized website brimming with information and images of the United States and U.S. history. The site includes information about historical events (such as the Vietnam War and Nazi Germany) that are interwoven with U.S. culture and memory.

HistoryChannel.com
http://www.historychannel.com

A comprehensive website for all ages, this site features a virtual classroom for grade-school students that includes tutorials and links related to content presented on The History Channel television network.

Houghton Mifflin Education Place
http://www.eduplace.com

This site includes numerous lesson plans for reading/language arts, science, social studies, and mathematics. It also provides sections for children and for parents, as well as for teacher professional development.

Humanities Text Initiative
http://www.hti.umich.edu

This website contains a digital library of historical documents. One example is the "Collected Works of Abraham Lincoln" which contains speeches, letters, advertisements, remarks, and much more.

Journey North
http://www.learner.org/jnorth

Sponsored by Annenberg/CPB this website presents a global study of wildlife migration for students in the United States and Canada. Includes reports of migration, tracking of migrations, classroom projects, and links to other tracking projects.

Kids as Global Scientists (KGS)
http://www.onesky.umich.edu/kgs01.html

This website offers a unique blend of structured weather curriculum, hands-on science investigations, and real-time information from the Internet. Students can access a number of resources, including weather-related activities and Internet-based weather maps.

Library of Congress
http://www.loc.gov

This website includes primary-source U.S. historical materials, including news articles, journals, and audio recordings of famous speeches. Click on "America's Library," where students can "Meet Amazing Americans," "Jump Back in Time," and "Explore the States."

Marshall Brain's How Stuff Works
http://www.howstuffworks.com

This website is a boon to anyone wanting to know the plain-language facts about how things such as computers, engines, and the human body work. The text is enhanced by clear illustrations and images.

NASA For Kids Only Earth Science Enterprise
http://kids.mtpe.hq.nasa.gov

Students will be introduced to how NASA studies air pollution, natural hazards, and other environmental topics. Students also can explore "Air," "Natural Hazards," "Land," and "Water" issues via this website.

National Geographic for Kids
http://www.nationalgeographic.com/kids

There is lots to see and do at this website. Students can learn about their world through games and activities, and teachers can use the site for teaching ideas for science, social studies, and geography.

National Park Service Links to the Past Cultural Resources
http://www.cr.nps.gov

This website provides activities for teaching about historic places in the United States and for exploring U.S. history. A drop-down menu lists many interesting topics. The site also includes tips for visiting these historic places.

North Carolina Department of Environment and Natural Resources Kid's Pages
http://www.ncfisheries.net/kids/index.html

This site contains fun student activities related to the environment. Kids can even learn how to fish here.

Rainforest Action Network: Kids' Corner
http://www.ran.org/ran/kids_action/index.html

This site contains activities about the rainforest, steps children can take to protect the environment, and lesson plans for teachers.

Ranger Rick's Kid Zone—National Wildlife Federation
http://www.nwf.org/kids

This website for children includes educational resources, including information on wetlands, endangered species, games, and a reader's corner.

Scholastic.com
http://teacher.scholastic.com

Fun activities for students and teachers can be found on this website. Students can write in different genres (such as biographies, journal entries, and book reviews) and work with a Scholastic editor. Or, students can study a number of topics such as science and current events. There are suggestions for teachers and parents as well.

Sea World/Busch Gardens Animal Information Database
http://www.seaworld.org

This site includes free online teacher's guides by grade level for topics such as whales, water animals, and fish. There is also a database of information about and pictures of different animals.

Sports Illustrated for Kids
http://www.sikids.com

A good website for children that contains current sports information and news, as well as games, sports trivia, and information on fantasy sports leagues.

U.S. National Archives & Records Administration
http://www.nara.gov

This site contains archived materials for students K–12 to use as they study U.S. history. The presidential libraries contain biographies, school projects, online documents, and interesting links.

WhitehouseKids.gov
http://www.whitehouse.gov/kids/index.html

This website includes the "Freedom Timeline," which features interesting stories about important events in U.S. history. In addition, site viewers can read biographies about the President, First Lady, Vice President, and Vice President's wife, and children are given information by the White House pets.

Windows to the Universe
http://www.windows.ucar.edu

A fascinating website specializing in earth and space sciences, this site includes tie-ins to history, art, and world culture as they pertain to earth and space sciences. The site contains an enormous amount of useful information that is ranked for the beginner, intermediate, or advanced researcher.

World Wildlife Fund Kids' Stuff
http://worldwildlife.org/fun/kids.cfm

Here children will find information on endangered species, protecting wildlife, and biodiversity. The site also includes educational resources and online activities for students.

News Websites

Boston.com—*Boston Globe*
http://www.globe.com
> This is the online edition of the *Boston Globe*. Students can access the day's news as well as the various sections of the newspaper.

CTNow.com—*Hartford Courant*
http://ctnow.com
> Newspaper articles listed by city are available at this site, and news is updated throughout the day.

The Internet Public Library—Online Newspapers
http://www.ipl.org/reading/news
> Readers can select a country and read news from around the world.

The New York Times Learning Network
http://www.nytimes.com/learning
> Sponsored by *The New York Times*, this website contains current news, lesson plans, and activities for students.

Yahooligans
http://yahooligans.com
> Click on News at this site, and find daily news on science, sports, U.S. news, and world news of interest to students.

Miscellaneous Websites for Students

KidsCom
http://www.kidscom.com
> This website includes craft and instructions for games that can be played online. This is a good site for teaching how to read and write instructional text.

Pen Pals

Kid City Post Office
http://www.child.net/kcpo.htm
> This free website is designed for students under the age of 13 who wish to find an e-mail pen pal (male or female). Students post an advertisement for an e-mail pen pal, so other students can read the ad and respond. The site includes rules for safely corresponding on the Internet.

The Kids on the Web: Pen Pals
http://www.zen.org/~brendan/kids-pen.html
> At this website, there are 22 links to other websites through which children and classrooms can communicate with others around the world. There are also links for English language learners and gifted students.

Peggy George's KeyPal Links

http://coe.west.asu.edu/scout/keypal.html

>This website lists 21 links to other "key pal" websites, which connect children with other children around the world via e-mail.

Advice Columns

Girl Scouts of America—Just 4 Girls

http://jfg.girlscouts.org

>"Ask Dr. M" offers advice about family, friends, and school. Girls can type in a problem and a question, click, and send it to Dr. M. The Just 4 Girls site also contains helpful resources about careers, how things work, fun and fitness, and arts and reading.

Travel

Most U.S. states have websites designed for children. The following list is a sampling:

The District

http://www.thedistrict.com

>This website includes travel tips as well as information about and links to the most popular attractions in Washington, D.C., including the Washington Monument, the Smithsonian Air and Space Museum, the White House, and the Lincoln Memorial.

Minnesota Office of Tourism—Explore Minnesota

http://www.exploreminnesota.com

>This website was designed for the general public interested in visiting Minnesota. In "Destination Areas" you can click on a specific area of the state (for example, Twin Cities) to find out more about that area's attractions, theatre, museums, lodging, and things to do.

Ohio Tourism—Kids' Stuff

http://www.OhioTourism.com/kids

>This website is designed with areas such as "Discover Ohio," "Visitor Information," "Games," and "GOAL (Great Ohio Adventures in Learning)."

TerraQuest

http://www.terraquest.com

>An informative and well-organized website that offers virtual exhibits and written accounts of travel in Antarctica, the Galapagos Islands, and Yosemite National Park.

Visiting Utah

http://utah.gov/learning/kidspage.html

>This website includes all the travel information for visiting Utah, and has special sites for children, including "History for Kids" and "State Symbols."

Index

Note: Page numbers followed by *f* indicate figures.

E

F

G

H

I

J

N

O

P

T

U–V

W–Z